Advanced Praise for *Love·*

"Imagine the wave of change that would wash over the country if every leader adopted Dr. Maria Church's model!"
— DEB NICHOLSON, author of *She Never Knew*, and editor of the Chesapeake Real Producers magazine

"Finally, a leadership model one can wrap her arms around! Dr. Church brings to light the real qualities of true leadership based on the very foundation of love, honor, and respect for one's fellow man (and woman). Her ability to guide others on this journey of self-discovery for the authentic leader within is a gift to all. After embracing LBL, one can't help but realize, with perfect clarity, the benefits of going for a walk."
— MARCELINA WERNE, R.N., C.E.O., Horizon Health Care Institute, LLC

"The timing for Dr. Maria Church's Love-Based Leadership (LBL) model for business leaders could not be more appropriate. With the country coming out of crisis and the labor force wounded and skeptical, this model of leadership will attract the best employees looking for a safe and caring environment under which to work."
— MICHAEL G. CEREPANYA, president, MGC Consulting, LLC

"Through her writings, her teachings, and most of all her contagiously enthusiastic actions, Dr. Maria Church reminds us that service, particularly public service, is not diminished by, but rather is made possible through a genuine love for self, those served, and 'the Why' that brings the two together. Everything becomes so much easier and more rewarding when you focus on loving yourself enough to be you at your best and loving others enough to do whatever you can to help them achieve the same. Contrary to what fear-based approaches would have us believe, facts aren't lost in love-based leadership. In fact, if we are willing to let ourselves be vulnerable, the truth of who we are and our experiences is illuminated, the connection to those we serve and their needs is created, and in that intersection lies the place for both hope and opportunity."

— MARYELLEN SHEPPARD, MAOM, SPHR, CPM;
human resources director, Pinal County, AZ;
assistant county manager, Maricopa County, AZ (retired)

"*Love-Based Leadership* has taught me that leading with heart and love fosters a work environment where authenticity, growth, and collaboration flourish. Focusing on skills, listening, and respect, I was able to develop and communicate my vision, and then support my team as they owned and ran with that vision. I am eternally grateful to Maria and her work for showing me how to become the leader I want to be and how to develop and support the best in myself and my team."

— SHAUNA MCISAAC, MD

LOVE-BASED LEADERSHIP

COMPLETELY REVISED
10th ANNIVERSARY EDITION
AND UPDATED

LOVE-BASED LEADERSHIP

THE MODEL FOR LEADING WITH STRENGTH, GRACE, AND AUTHENTICITY

DR. MARIA CHURCH

DUDLEY COURT PRESS
SONOITA, AZ

Published in the United States of America by
Dudley Court Press
PO Box 102 Sonoita, AZ 85637
www.DudleyCourtPress.com

Cover and interior design by Dunn+Associates, www.Dunn-Design.com

Publisher's Cataloging-in-Publication Data
Names: Church, Maria, 1961- author.

Title: Love-based leadership : the model for leading with strength, grace,
and authenticity / Dr. Maria Church.

Description: 10th anniversary edition, completely revised and updated.
Sonoita, Arizona : Dudley Court Press, [2020]
First edition issued by Balboa Press, 2010. | Includes bibliographical references.

Identifiers: ISBN: 978-1-940013-67-1 (paper)
978-1-940013-68-8 (EBook)
978-1-940013-69-5 (audio)
LCCN: 2020915924

Subjects:
LCSH: Leadership. | Authentic leadership. | Business communication. | Success.Success in business.
Love--Psychological aspects. | Love—Social aspects. | Self-acceptance. | Self- actualization (Psychology)
BISAC: BUSINESS & ECONOMICS / Business Communication / General. | BUSINESS & ECONOMICS / Leadership.
SELF-HELP / Personal Growth / Success.

Classification: LCC: HD57.7 .C48 2020
DDC: 658.4/092--dc23

For Brian.
I will love you 'til the stars
fall from the sky.

Contents

Contents

Foreword

"Love" is not a word that is used often in professional settings, yet we say it freely everywhere else. We love our families, of course, and our pets; our hometowns and our home teams. When love does come up in our professional lives, it's usually in the context of loving—or not—the work we do.

I have spent my career in local governments across four states, including the last 15 years as the city manager in Fort Collins, Colorado, and I do love my work. It has also become abundantly clear to me through the years that building a community requires love beyond the work itself. It requires a deep love for the community, for the people and businesses in it, and for my colleagues who are equally passionate about this form of public service.

I first met Maria Church several years ago when we were both speaking at an Alliance for Innovation conference in Phoenix. As we learned more about the work the other was doing, we discovered that our leadership philosophies are very much aligned. She has proven an invaluable resource in this space, and her research and teaching captures so much about the ways we are trying to lead in Fort Collins.

Her message of leading from love instead of fear resonates deeply. Like many leaders I confess that earlier in my career I sometimes approached my work with a harsher, all-business tone. As I've grown in my own leadership journey, I've come to understand that how we do our work matters just as much as the work itself. Leading with genuine care for others and ourselves is the best way for any organization to achieve the results it is working toward.

Sometimes when I talk to various work groups across my organization—police patrol officers, perhaps, or a street or utility field crew—this notion of loving our colleagues meets some initial resistance. After all, traditional professional language doesn't typically go there. But as Dr. Church explains, if we can easily talk about loving our families, friends and neighbors, I don't think it's at all a stretch to talk about loving our colleagues, too. We spend the majority of our waking hours with our co-workers—of course those relationships matter! I know I wouldn't last very long in a job where the human interactions were purely transactional.

It is apt that Dr. Church's book is being re-released in 2020, and I cannot think of a year that we need this message of love-based leadership more. In just a few months we have endured a global pandemic and the ensuing economic fallout, a reckoning around systemic racism and police accountability, and the effects of climate change through devastating hurricane and wildfire seasons—not to mention a highly contentious presidential election still to come. It is quite a collection of traumas for us to live through, much less lead through. When the world recovers and economies begin to thrive again, the way we treated our people during these difficult times will be critical in determining our longer-term success or failure as leaders.

Throughout this book Dr. Church makes clear that the traditional, fear-based approach to leadership is the very antithesis of love. Leading via fear is easy—it's been modeled throughout history and we've all experienced it in our lives.

It's also not working anymore. It does not win allies, does not foster a positive organizational culture, and does not inspire others to work toward a shared vision. Anyone who is still using a fear-based leadership framework must adapt, and quickly. Continuing to motivate through manipulation, operate from a scarcity mentality, and wield honesty as a weapon simply will not take you where you want to go. Fortunately, Dr. Church has offered us a path forward.

In this year when so much is beyond our control, it can be tempting to grasp for what we can control and revert to leading from a place of power and fear. But there is enough fear in the world right now. What has gotten us through 2020 and will continue to guide us forward is our human connection and care for one another. When the world is scary, what is most needed in our dialogue is love.

My hope is that above all, Dr. Church's message will inspire each of us to stay curious—about ourselves, our colleagues and our purpose, and about how we can lead better by loving better.

Darin Atteberry
City Manager
Fort Collins, Colorado

Preface to the 10th Anniversary Edition

As I begin the work on the 10th Anniversary Edition of *Love-Based Leadership*, I realize that I have the same paralysis as I did when I wrote the first edition. I find myself in the middle of the COVID-19 crisis plagued with love, fear, hope, sadness, relief, anticipation, creativity, and a myriad of other emotions—all in the same short span of an hour. How do I write about leading with love when I sit in sadness or fear? Yesterday, I had to drop off some papers for my husband at work. He was at his office, as he provides an essential service. Driving through our small rural community, I was struck with the eerie sight of carless parking lots and closed businesses. A wall of sadness enveloped me while tears blinded my ability to see. So many hopes of business owners have evaporated or, worse, turned into dark clouds of broken dreams and mounting debt.

Later that day, I watched one of my clients, a city manager of a nearby municipality, deliver his first virtual employee town hall to thousands of worried employees. When asked if the city was planning layoffs, he valiantly and loving said that he did not know.

How can I write about *leading* with love, when I don't know where we are going?

What I do know is that in times of crisis, we look to leadership to answer:

1. Where are we headed?

2. How are we going to get there?

3. How is the leader going to get us there and keep us safe?

Just as the city manager honestly stated, I too do not know exactly where we are headed. I do know that we are in a state of chaos, which means we are in a state of reorganizing matter. I do know that we get to help shape what that reorganization of matter looks like. I do know that if we shape it from a place of love instead of fear, that place will be much more desirable and life-giving.

How are we going to get there? I do know for sure that in order to get to a place that is better than before COVID-19, we must do so with intention and strategy. Mindfulness in how we get there is more important than ever before. We need to be proactive in this strategy of creating a new way of living. If we don't, then someone else will.

How are we, as leaders, going to keep our families, loved ones, teams, and communities safe? Again, we must approach the answers to these questions with mindfulness and purpose. We are already seeing neighborhood leaders checking on other neighbors, offering to grocery shop for older or at-risk people, as well as sewing circles making masks for health-care workers.

The times remind me of old war movies where communities band together to support the war effort in any way necessary—and often in ways that are not part of our regular routines or comfort zones. Organizations are putting together quick skills matrices to see who can help in an area that needs it. This is far different from usual tasks. Parks and Recreation employees are now manning help lines for constituents. An HR director at another county is working in the prison because she had law enforcement experience in her early career. Retired nurses are coming out of retirement to help care for the sick.

What we see is Love-Based Leadership at its best. This gives me hope for crafting our new normal. My hope is further fueled by seeing top-end clothing designers making masks, a high-end hair dryer manufacturer making respirators, luxury airlines delivering medical supplies, and private flying clubs becoming pop-up sewing rooms for protective masks.

Creativity abounds as artists, entrepreneurs, and educators are developing alternative mediums to educate, inspire, and entertain. Yes, Love-Based Leadership at its best.

After deep reflection, I've decided to completely update this book. Love-Based Leadership is growing and timely. One of the changes you will find in this **10th Anniversary Edition** is a new chapter on Creating a Love-Based Organizational Culture. The work that my team and I have been doing to create love-based cultures is exciting, and I believe this information will be valuable to you as well. Three new chapters go into the model in more depth. I've also added a quick reference guide to see at a glance the twenty-one factors of Love-Based Leadership. In celebration of the ten years of teaching and witnessing Love-Based Leadership in action, I've put together an honorary workbook for you from my Love-Leader Matrix,™ which you can download from LoveLeaderMatrix.com. An afterword note is also included to capture some of the exciting work that has been done in the last ten years incorporating love into leadership and into the workplace.

Love is in the air, and I pray that it is here to stay . . .

With love,
Maria
April 2020
www.DrMariaChurch.com

Preface to the 2010 Edition

Lao Tzu said, "The journey of a thousand miles begins with a single step." I began with that phrase as a motivator to start the writing process; however, I realized it is also the key to becoming a great leader. I have thought about this book for several years and have been afraid to begin. "Why are you afraid?" you may ask. I'm not entirely sure of the answer, but I believe it may parallel the trepidation and myriad of emotions I experienced when completing my dissertation. Moving from the status of student to doctor comes with some built-in pressure. Perhaps the pressure is my own, which is bad enough. There is an expectation. When I crossed over to writer/author—yikes, talk about pressure! Many thoughts, fears, and anxieties ran through my head and contributed to my paralysis: *What if I fail? What if I don't fail? Will I be able to make a good living? Will I inspire leaders and managers in a positive way? Will I help change the way we look at care, love, and trust in the workplace? Will people take the message seriously? What if I write with the true passion of my soul? I will bare my soul in writing, a forever format. Will my soul be cherished or trashed?*

Well, honey, you can't swim if you don't get in the water. Leadership: What is it? How is it defined? Two great questions. Two reasonable questions. Two thousand responses. In my experience, the words leadership and management are used interchangeably in the workplace. In the management and leadership classes I've taught over the years, we define them differently.

Many organizations use the term "leader" when defining certain management positions. A title does not make a leader. My grandpa Jaime used to say, "You can put a suit on a bum, but he is still a bum." One may put the title of leader on a person, and he or she may or may not be a leader.

Most definitions of leadership have one overarching similarity: vision. Creating vision and motivating followers toward the vision is the fundamental basis of leadership. If there is no place to lead (vision) and no one to follow, then leadership is absent. I define leadership as the action of inspiring and motivating others toward a vision. I don't believe it needs to be any more complicated than that.

Leading and being a leader has its pressure, too. With the title comes an expectation. That's where some would-be leaders fail, not living up to the expectation of what it means to be a leader. When we force leadership to emerge, as when we force anything (love, money, praise), it isn't natural and sincere. So why do we force it?

Then there is the whole debate of whether leaders are born or made and whether one can learn how to be a leader. I emphatically answer yes to both. I have known many people in my life who seem like natural leaders who didn't even realize their leadership skills. I've also known people who didn't have any obvious leadership qualities but were then able to grow into wonderful leaders with the desire to learn the tools and dedication to complete the necessary work.

What would happen if we didn't force leadership to emerge? What if we just focused on finding the leader within? Finding the leader within is only as difficult as we make it. For some, it's a difficult proposition. For others, the self-exploration is fun. Many of us have known the leader within to be there and have been waiting for the opportunity to let it out.

This doesn't need to be a drastic escape; it can be slow and maybe even go unnoticed at first. When we let the leader out—the true, authentic leader within—others will notice.

Use this book as a workbook as you explore your own leadership and take time to be reflective. Bend the edges. Highlight what resonates with you. Write your notes in the margins. Each chapter ends with an invitation to take a walk, reflect, and determine how you may put into action the leadership model presented throughout these pages.

Welcome, and thank you for taking this journey toward discovering your authentic leader, the leader others want to follow. You are not alone in this journey; we will travel together.

In love,
Maria
August 2010

Introduction

Meaning

Why start another book about leadership? The answer is simple. Because we want more. Not necessarily more leadership books, but more out of life. We want more from our leaders. We want more from our work. We want more from our personal lives, and we want more from our spiritual lives. But more what? More challenges, rewards, money, recognition, fulfillment, joy, honesty, care, abundance, time, and meaning.

That's why this book on leadership is important. Leadership is a conduit to meaning. Leadership inspires others toward vision. Leadership is necessary in our lives; it's everywhere. Many of us follow leaders at work, or we lead at work. Leadership abounds in our communities. Leadership is ubiquitous in our personal lives and in our families as well.

While we look for more meaning in our lives at work, home, and play, until we begin to find that meaning, we are unsettled. Did you ever notice how challenges in our lives cause us to ask, *Why?* We ask because we want to make sense of the situation. We want to understand the meaning behind the event so we can move on. When we don't find meaning, we become disillusioned, lack motivation, and find substitutes for meaningful experiences. Sometimes we choose unhealthy or destructive substitutes. Some of us go through the motions and become human doings instead of human beings. Some of us succumb to overwhelming stress when we believe we are living a meaningless life. Even worse, some of us give up on life when we perceive our lives to lack meaning.

I remember a discussion I had with the general manager of a regional division on the topic of the importance of finding meaning in work for our employees and leaders. His response was, "I think meaning at work is overrated." Overrated? We spend the vast majority of our adult lives at work. One of the primary purposes of a leader is to inspire vision and motivation in those he or she leads. Few things are more inspiring and motivating than meaningful work.

Love

"Love? You cannot write about love; no one would understand it. People will be confused by the word love." I heard those words repeatedly as I continued interviewing professors for my dissertation committee. I could hardly believe my ears. No one would understand love? What sort of culture are we that we no longer understand love?

It became a mission of one of the faculty chairs to make sure the rest of the faculty would discourage my desire to write about this new model of leadership. The ironic part of this experience was the encouragement I received from my cohort as I was developing the model. They all supported it and believed the time was right to introduce this leadership model. Finally, when I was insistent and descriptive about my passion in developing this new model of leadership, a professor told me to wait until I had "Dr." in front of my name to introduce the model. I begrudgingly accepted the fact that support from the university to pursue this as my dissertation was not forthcoming. Now is the time to introduce you to Love-Based Leadership (LBL).

I found it both interesting and curious that some thought the word love would confuse people. Some said people would think it's sexual. Do we always associate love with sex? I believe we are too intelligent a species to make that exclusive association. To understand love at a deeper level, let's first look at the antithesis of love: fear.

Fear is almost as powerful as love, and certainly easier to fall into for many of us. Fear is distrust, disbelief, and ignorance. Historically, fear has been a powerful means of motivating others. Fear has moved the masses into action or retreat. Fear has moved multitudes of people to non-action and apathy. Fear is a formidable force. Yet fear can leave as quickly as the snap of a finger.

In this book, we explore the fundamental elements of Love-Based Leadership (LBL): why it's important in our organizations and how to develop those skills and traits. We face fear head-on, and we open up the power of choice in our lives.

The journey to leadership must start within. We need to go inward, allowing reflection and introspection to develop our own leadership skills and qualities. I invite you to step into a space of self-reflection at specific times throughout the book with the invitation: *Let's Go for a Walk.* This is your time to go inward, to think, to be present in the moment, and to reflect on your own leadership. Over the years, when working with many different people I often suggest that we go for a walk to clear our heads, relieve our stress, regroup, and take time for introspection. Grab your journal or notebook and a pen and let's get moving.

How Did We Get Here?

Water is fluid, soft, and yielding. But water will wear away rock, which is rigid and cannot yield. As a rule, whatever is fluid, soft, and yielding will overcome whatever is rigid and hard. This is another paradox: what is soft is strong.

— Lao-Tzu (600 B.C.)

Have a strong mind and a soft heart.

— Anthony J. D'Angelo

chapter 1

Meaning

A few years ago, I wrote a reflective piece entitled "I Have Arrived." The following is an excerpt:

> *I've done it! I accomplished whatever Mom and Dad told me I could do! I have arrived.*
>
> *As the firstborn of a pre-baby boomer couple, my parents always told me to do what makes me happy and remember that I could accomplish anything. They supported my desire to pursue acting. They supported my desire to study sign language interpretation (I liked the dramatic flair), then they encouraged my business drive. My mother always had a career. She broke through many glass ceilings and earned great respect in her profession. She was my inspiration to break on through to the other side. I have arrived.*
>
> *When I moved up in my organization and took on more responsibility, I tripled my income over a nine-month period. In addition to the money, I earned respect and a place at the table*

with the men. Four men and little ol' me. I had a place at the table in a predominately all-male industry. I have arrived.

I changed my wardrobe, hair, and personal style. After all, I was in senior management. I have arrived.

I worked eighty hours a week. I was dealing in hundreds of thousands of dollars daily. I was getting little sleep with the worry. Yet, I felt important and needed. The men in my organization had come to depend on me and my opinion. I have arrived.

I started to show symptoms of extreme stress. On my fortieth birthday, the doctor put me on blood pressure medicine and told me I needed to exercise more. I'd been working long hours, and my eating habits were atrocious. Fast food eaten even faster became the norm. I took up smoking as a stress reliever (yes, I am an educated woman, and yes, I know the hazards of smoking). I have arrived.

One day on my back patio after a long day at work, with a martini in one hand and a cigarette in the other, I had a thought: I have a place at the table. I have earned respect for my hard work and knowledge. I have an awesome six-figure income. I have everything the successful men have had for decades. I have

thirty pounds. I have a high-level position. I
have a stressful job. I have a beautiful home. I
have high blood pressure. I have a drink in one
hand and a cigarette in the other. Oh my God
. . . I do have it all! I have arrived . . .

But just exactly where am I?

Funny, isn't it, how the quest for success, if it has no lasting meaning, is meaningless. Searching for answers and
reflecting on meaning in our life is a mysterious, ominous
quest and has been the lifework of many artists, poets,
scientists, philosophers, and scholars. The pursuit of finding meaning is a challenge for many organizations today,
evidenced by unhealthy organizational cultures, dysfunc-
tional work environments, high turnover, and financial
losses. Work-related illness due to stress is on the rise. These
may be categorized by both physical and psychosocial
illnesses. Heart disease, diabetes, digestive disorders, high
blood pressure, chronic back pain, substance abuse, and
anxiety disorders are just some of the work-related illness
that are harming us. Leaders and employees' work have
become joyless striving[1], finding no meaning in the work
done eight to ten hours a day. The job of leadership is to
inspire and motivate others toward a vision. If we don't
see or believe in the mission, we don't have meaning and
we don't have full commitment from our employees. To
borrow a phrase from the restaurant industry, we just have
"butts in seats."

So many books have been written on the quest for finding
meaning. Dr. Viktor Frankl's *Man's Search for Meaning*[2]

tops my list. Frankl believed that men and women are *meaning-seeking animals*. His theoretical model, Logotherapy, doesn't look at what's wrong, but rather, what's right, what has meaning, and what we want to do in our life that has meaning for us. Frankl describes three ways to discover the meaning of life: (1) by creating a work or doing a deed, (2) by experiencing something or encountering someone, and (3) by the attitude taken toward unavoidable suffering.

Frankl's three modes to discover meaning are all applicable methods at work in our daily lives. Again, creating a work or deed, working for or with others, and keeping our attitudes in line are all opportunities for us to find meaningful daily experiences. While we spend the majority of our days at work, this is the place where we want to experience one or more of these approaches to finding meaning. We need to have these experiences as human beings, because as Frankl stated, we are meaning-seeking animals. We so often look to others, especially leadership, to inspire and stimulate us with those meaningful experiences. As leaders who want to leave a legacy, being a conduit to those meaningful experiences will leave a lasting impression.

Maslow's well-known and highly respected hierarchy of needs theory[3] describes five levels of needs based on three assumptions: (1) we are only motivated by unmet needs, (2) needs are hierarchical in nature, basic to complex, and (3) lower-level needs must be met before moving to higher-order needs. We will explore these needs later on in more detail, but for now, here are the needs in order of basic to complex:

1. Physiological needs—basic needs of air, food, water, shelter, sex, and relief/avoidance of pain.

2. Safety needs—after the basic needs are met, safety and security must be met.

3. Belongingness or social needs—after safety needs are met, we want to feel connections with people.

4. Esteem needs—after social needs are met, we desire self-respect, status, and recognition for our accomplishments.

5. Self-actualization needs—the highest level of need is the development of our full potential. To achieve this sense of fulfillment, we seek to understand and grow, to find meaning in our work and our lives.

Based on Maslow's hierarchy of needs from a work perspective, employees entering our workplaces will have physiological and safety needs met. Most people will not even apply for a job unless their basic needs such as food and shelter can be met. If the position will not pay enough for the rent/mortgage, food, or transportation to get to work, many people will not even apply. Regarding safety needs, people will typically not apply for a job if it is not "safe."

Safety in this context applies to both literal and figurative. Social sites such as Glassdoor, Indeed, and LinkedIn now give prospective employees a glimpse into organizations from employees' perspectives. With an entire generation that does not make buying decisions without checking reviews, why in the world would they choose to spend the vast majority of their working hours in an organization with poor ratings?

The third tier, belongingness and/or social needs, are the connections we crave with others. This is part of our DNA—we are tribal and clan oriented. Often after a certain period of time on the new job, we seek relationships with our work mates. Going to lunch, taking coffee breaks with each other, or perhaps a cocktail after work are all ways we fill these belongingness needs. This is an important need-level tier for us to pay attention to, since most of our employees enter at this need level. It is also a level where we lose employees.

Our esteem needs are when we desire recognition or respect from others. We want to know we are valued and appreciated. Leaders who are good at this are always remembered by employees, colleagues, and peers. We often remember how we felt when someone said something to or about us, rather than the specific words uttered by the person. How we felt about those statements or actions has a much longer duration and deeply affects us more than the actual words. I remember growing up hearing my mother repeating one of her favorite mantras, "Actions speak louder than words." How true, Mother, how very true. This is often the place that we lose good people at work, because they do not feel valued and honored. We've probably heard the phrase, "People don't leave jobs; they leave bosses." It is such a shame when we lose good people because we forgot to thank them, acknowledge their contribution, or honor them. Let's face it, recognizing employees costs nothing, and yet the ROI is priceless.

The highest level of needs is the one for self-actualization. This is where we seek, with a voracious hunger, to find meaning and purpose in what we do. Meeting this need is the fulfillment of meaning. People may leave organizations when they reach this need level because their work is not a conduit to their meaning-seeking behavior and needs. It is not unusual to hear of an executive with a sexy title who leaves a high-powered, high-paying position and moves to the country to live on a farm. They left because they were searching for meaningful work, meaningful contribution, and believing that a simpler life might provide that. We may start a new job and begin the quest of the hierarchical pyramid all over again, but we will eventually be right back to this higher order of need.

When we look at these two theories, a common theme emerges of meaning and love. Do we find meaning through love, or do we find love through meaning? I'm not sure we can have one without the other. Love is the conduit to meaning, purpose, and abundant living. Both theories are rooted in love: love of self and love of others.

We spend so much of our days at work, home, and play leading and being led by others. How do we find meaning in our leadership, and can we be a source for helping others find meaning through our leadership? Hmmm, to lead in a meaningful way . . .

We all leave a legacy—why not consciously create the legacy? Do you want someone else to define your legacy? Meaningfulness and self-actualization are feeling a part of something bigger—as big as a legacy.

The quest for something more is evident. Work-related illnesses are on the rise. Stress reduction workshops are everywhere. Evidence of people's desire for a more spiritual and holistic life is on grocery store shelves, on advertisements, and in kitchens and baths across America. Spiritual practices such as yoga, prayer, meditation, and aromatherapy, which are far from the practices that have guided American businesses since the eighteenth century, are creeping into offices and boardrooms. The evidence is there: *we want more.*

I invite you to discover a model of leadership that can help you realize meaning and strength, aiding you to inspire and motivate those around you in meaningful experiences. Let's be a part of something bigger.

A New Leadership Model

When I was in postgraduate school beginning work on my dissertation and interviewing faculty as potential committee members for my study, I described a model of leadership that I wanted to introduce into the great body of knowledge. After speaking with several professors, one of the deans spoke with me about my leadership model and told me that people wouldn't understand it. She told me that the word I was using would turn them off. I was shocked. I was disappointed and most profoundly, I was disillusioned. How could this word not be discussed in an advanced study of leadership? How could we talk and theorize about motivating and inspiring others without talking about this word? What did leadership mean? What did followership mean without this word? How could people not be drawn to this word and, even more shocking, how could this word be so powerful as to turn people off? What is this powerful, scary, misunderstood word?

Love.

Shocking, isn't it?

A leadership model based on love brought about that level of reaction. This isn't a new concept; we've seen many leaders throughout history lead with love and compassion. Some may refer to this type of leadership as servant leadership. Similar in some ways to servant leadership, Love-Based Leadership (LBL) goes beyond the follower focus to incorporate self-awareness and a holistic approach to our lives. LBL explores not only walking the talk but considers layers to the depths of meaning in our own leadership so we might help those we lead find meaningful experiences in their own lives.

I always chuckle when I hear people refer to love and compassion in relation to leadership as a *soft* skill. Those of us who have participated in love know there is nothing soft about it. It's hard, very hard. Love is our core as human beings. I remember feeling moved by the phone calls from passengers on those planes that were involved in the tragic and fatal terrorist acts on September 11, 2001. Several passengers on those planes telephoned their loved ones to proclaim their love. These passengers wanted to pass from this life in love, sharing love, and receiving love. "Love is not consolation. It is light," Nietzsche wrote. I believe in those words of Nietzsche's, and that the people on those planes wanted light and love as they passed from this world.

Definitions

Before we move along, allow me to contextualize definitions as they relate to this book.

Love brings to mind several varied interpretations, definitions, and constructs for different people. Definitions range from a kindness and fondness of others to sexual connotations. Plato carried love from the physical aspect to "an immaterial beauty such as justice, wisdom, and knowledge." For the purpose of this book, love is simply defined as knowledge, wisdom, and acceptance of one's authentic self and others. Synonyms of love include soul, spirit, and care.

Fear, equally powerful of evoking strong emotional constructs, is typically thought of as a reaction to something threatening. For the purpose of this book, fear is defined as an immobilizing emotion of uncertainty beyond one's conscience control. Synonyms of fear include anxiety and ego.

Source is the Higher Power, Universal Power, Creator, and/ or God, also referred to as Yahweh, Allah, and the Buddha.

Let's Go for a Walk

"Your vision will be clear only when you look into your heart . . . Who looks outside, dreams. Who looks inside awakens."

— *Carl Jung*

Consider this our wake-up call. Effective leadership begins first with one's self. We must go inward and be authentic leaders with ourselves first before we can be an authentic, effective leader of others. Think about the times you traveled and listened to the instruction of the flight attendants as they described what would happen if the plane were to lose air pressure in the cabin: Oxygen masks will drop down. If you are traveling with a child or someone who may need assistance, you must first put the oxygen mask on yourself. Then and only then do you lead someone else to oxygen.

Let's break and take this opportunity to go inward—to stop and think about how the contents in this chapter resonate with you.

- What is meaningful to you?
- What inspires you?
- When was the last time you listened to your heart?

Reflection: What is meaningful to you?

Reflection: What inspires you?

Reflection: When was the last time you listened to your heart?

chapter 2

Where Have All the Leaders Gone?

While conducting research of books on leadership when I first wrote this book ten years ago, I found over 62,000 titles on Amazon. Ten years later, Amazon lists over 80,000 books on leadership. Thousands of leadership-related professional organizations abound with many types of leadership programs. Businesses, nonprofits, governments, and local chambers of commerce all across America have leadership programs. Why is there so much interest in leadership?

Three reasons come to mind. First, as a workforce, we're disillusioned with the state of so-called leadership today. Looking at the downfall of Enron, the irresponsibility of BP Oil, the physical force used by United Airlines with a customer on an overbooked flight, the carelessness of Equifax security measures resulting in a breach of 148 million consumers, country divisiveness, and the collapse of our economy is cause for pause. Social, political, economic, religious, and educational structures have fractured and are broken. Second, a population of over seventy-six million baby boomers (born between 1946 and 1964) continue to retire. Compare that to only sixty-five million workers of the Generation X population, and we can see the serious gap of talent, experience, and organizational leadership this deficit brings.

For the most compelling reason we need good leadership, one simply has to turn on the news and see economic comparisons of today (2010 and 2020!) correlated to those of the Great Depression. It's not my intention here to debate that statement. It is my intention to recognize the magnitude of unemployed people and the COVID-19 disruption of business, recreation, and homes. Many of our neighbors and friends are reeling from the effects of joblessness. While the financial aspects of joblessness are profound, we must not neglect the emotional and behavioral ways this crisis has affected the currently employed workforce, the unemployed workforce, and how it will continue to affect the workforce as they reenter companies and organizations. This was true in 2010 and even more relevant today, in 2020.

Those people still employed today are doing the jobs of three to four people, with no additional pay, and in many cases, less pay than a few years ago. A common philosophy in organizations is *you are lucky to have a job*. The still employed have become disillusioned, overworked, and have no sense of loyalty to the organizations where they work. Employees have little to no trust in their employers because they have seen many coworkers laid off. The unemployed have gone through feelings of betrayal, devaluation, and mistrust with corporate America.

As the economy recovers and jobless rates decrease, there will be movement in and among organizations. Many of those people who stuck it out in their jobs during the downturn in the economy will leave as more job opportunities become available. Those unemployed who will reenter the job market will do so with great trepidation. Strategies must be in place to retain and attract the talent, experience, and in-demand workers.

In 2010, I shared information from the Society for Human Resource Management (SHRM)[4] that surveyed employees looking for new jobs outside of their current organization. Nearly two thirds of those workers were leaving because they did not feel valued. The top three reasons were 1) lack of open communication, 2) no opportunities to balance life, and 3) lack of meaningful work. Unfortunately, not much has changed. According to the *Retention Report*[5], the three top specific reasons for employees to leave jobs in 2017 were career development (21 percent), work-life balance (13 percent), and manager behavior (11 percent). Employers are still not meeting employee expectations and needs. My experience of working with organizations over the past ten years confirms these findings.

When organizations are not forthcoming with information and lack open employee communication, an air of distrust and a feeling of unimportance is present in the minds of employees. Nearly every organization with whom I work consistently tells me about their top two challenges: communication and trust. Employees just want leaders to be honest and open and to remember that open communication does not go in only one direction—it must go both ways. Employees also want their voices heard and acknowledged for the value and information they bring to the table.

On several occasions, an employer of mine would bring consultants in to do studies on our marketplace. We were a local homebuilder and knew our market well. The company headquarters were in another state, and the corporate leadership would bring out-of-state consultants in to do the studies. The consultants would obtain all of their information about our buyers, including buyer profiles from the sales and marketing team, put it into a report with a pretty cover, charge the annual salary of one receptionist, and submit it to our corporate office. Corporate would then rave about the results. The sales and marketing employees felt devalued. What a waste of resources as well when the staff already had the information but were not tapped into by corporate for their knowledge and expertise. Leveraging the experience and knowledge of the local staff, the company could have saved a significant amount of money, used valuable information, and reinforced the value and appreciation of the sales and marketing team. A win-win situation could have occurred for all.

When we bring back unemployed workers and want to retain current workers, demonstrating employee value will be crucial. We show employee value by establishing a trusting relationship when we communicate and demonstrate honor and trust to each other. Workers will inevitably reenter the marketplace with a lack of trust. Why is it so important for our employees to trust us? Without trust, you will not have full buy-in and commitment from your employees.

Without trust, you will not have knowledge creation. Without knowledge creation, you will not have a business. Lack of trust is a major issue inside organizations, and it is costing them a lot of money. *Harvard Business Review* reported that 58% of people say they trust strangers more than their boss.[6] We let strangers drive our children home from practice in Uber and Lyft, yet we do not trust our bosses.

Employees need to feel that it's not only satisfactory to express their opinions, questions, and feelings, but that it's encouraged and necessary, all the while trusting that their environment is a safe place in which to do so. Organizations want to be innovative and creative. Without trust, it is impossible to grow, develop, and innovate. Trust is a foundation to learning and innovation.

When the economy begins to recover, employers will want to attract and retain the best employees. To do this, employers must make their organizations desirable. What makes a workplace desirable? When we look at Maslow's hierarchy of needs, we learn that employees first look for their basic needs for food and shelter. The next tier is safety. This refers to both literal and figurative safety. Most organizations are literally safe due to OSHA guidelines. Figurative safety represents how "safe" (think secure) this position may be. Does the organization receive a high Glassdoor rating, or is rapid turnover prevalent? Is there harassment or bullying? Is this potential new job a short-term position paid under a grant or short-term contract? These factors play into the safe decision to potentially work for an organization. Typically, you won't have an employee join an organization if they perceive that their basic needs or safety needs won't be met. Or if they thought their needs would be met, only to find that wasn't the case, they would leave shortly after their arrival. I know of several organizations, including many of my clients, who put their Glassdoor ratings front and center on their websites to let prospective employees know that their company is a great place to work.

After safety needs, we crave belongingness. These needs are met in both healthy work cultures and unhealthy work environments. Employees in healthy work environments feel connected to their colleagues through collaboration, creation, and problem solving. Oftentimes, coworkers become friends, which solidifies their work relationships even more. In unhealthy work cultures, employees often band together for survival. They commiserate about their state of affairs and daydream together about how it could be better. Workers in an unhealthy environment often spend their time planning their escape from the current organization to one that may be healthier or more aligned with their needs.

In unhealthy work cultures, some employees may never feel the sense of belongingness because of mistrust. Sometimes, we don't feel a sense of belonging because the culture is too closed and not welcoming of new people into their circle. Or worse yet, you may only join the circle if you change who you are to become more like the inner-circle members. None of these scenarios demonstrates love for you, your uniqueness, or your value. This need level on the hierarchy is often a point when employees exit an organization. A red flag indicating that an employee may leave the organization at this need level is when they get their belongingness needs met outside of the workplace. "I can't stand this job/department/organization, but I love the people I work with" is a telltale sign that the employee may soon be leaving the organization.

After belongingness needs, employees have the need for recognition. Recognition can occur in both healthy and unhealthy work cultures. The difference is the perceived sincerity of the employees when recognition is given. Additionally, not meeting this recognition need, coupled with the employee not feeling appreciated, almost certainly guarantees that the employee will look elsewhere to meet those needs. Each time an employee looks somewhere besides work to fill a need, they become that much less engaged and less committed to their workplace. Eventually, the worker will leave to find an employer that does appreciate and recognize them and their contribution to the organization. This hierarchical need level is also an exit point for many workers. A red flag may be comments such as, "I'm not appreciated around here" or "I need to go elsewhere where my opinions count."

The final need is for self-actualization. Employers desire and covet in their employees the eight behaviors demonstrated at this highest level of the hierarchy. First, concentration is sharper. Maslow defined self-actualization as "experiencing fully, vividly, selflessly, with full concentration and total absorption" in his last book, *The Farther Reaches of Human Nature*.[7]

Next, growth choices are another behavior of a self-actualized individual. This is when we must choose comfort or growth. We know people who do not leave where they are no matter how unhappy they may be because they are comfortable in the familiar. To grow and stretch is scary for some of us. I knew this firsthand when I made the decision to leave the comfort of my decade-long, six-figure income. For me, the choice was either to grow or to stagnate and die. Growing pains is a term that describes this transition well, as it was painful to make the change. However, when I refocused on the reasons, I chose growth over comfort in my quest for self-actualization. I had razor-sharp focus and boundless creativity.

*Only through awareness
can we move to understanding.*

Self-awareness is the third behavior demonstrated by a self-actualized person. With self-awareness, we recognize our own strength and power. We are also uncomfortable with certain behaviors and attitudes we recognize in ourselves. As leaders, developing our self-awareness is crucial. This ongoing activity helps us understand ourselves and gain a better understanding of others. Only through awareness can we move to understanding. With understanding, we can move to acceptance. When we accept not only ourselves but others for their humanness, we can have an environment ripe for love.

Honesty, the fourth behavior, is ubiquitous in self-actualization. How can we not be honest if we begin a path of self-awareness and growth? Honesty is a behavior that most employers look for when hiring. We desire honesty, but many people don't always like to hear the truth. Two unhealthy patterns have developed in the workplace. One phenomenon I have observed over and over again is an employee telling the boss what the employee believed the boss wanted to hear (whether it was true or not). Not being honest with those whom you work will come back to bite you. Dishonesty never wins in the end. It may win for a period of time, but not ultimately.

Another unhealthy pattern veiled as honesty I've witnessed is when people use the banner of "I'm just being honest" to belittle, criticize, and dehumanize others. Being honest is not an excuse to be ugly. Honesty is a virtue, not a weapon. What happened to good manners? As we evolve and become more sophisticated, do we no longer need manners? When honesty is used as a weapon, all trust immediately dissipates.

Judgment is the fifth behavior demonstrated in self-actualization. Our judgment skills become sharp and fine-tuned in conjunction with the other seven behaviors at this point in the hierarchy. Who doesn't want an employee with good judgment?

The sixth behavior is self-development. Completely aligned with continued learning and knowledge acquisition, self-development is a win-win behavior for both the employee and the organization with which they work. Like self-development, self-actualization is not an arrival. It is a never-ending, ongoing process contributing meaning to our lives.

Peak experiences are the seventh behavior of a self-actualized individual. This is when we are acutely aware of our wholeness and connection with others. We think, act, and feel with more clarity, allowing us to love and accept others without anxiety or conflict. Often referred to as *Aha!* moments, we feel most alive in our peak experiences.

Finally, a lack of ego defense leads our way to self-actualization. We are able to recognize our ego defenses and distortions on reality, release them, and see with sharper clarity.

If we could lead workers who did not succumb to ego, who took the initiative for self-development, who had stronger awareness, honesty, judgment, growth, and concentration, we might even say that leadership is easy. These are all characteristics that comprise an awesome workgroup. I would certainly want to lead a group of employees with these skills, traits, and behaviors.

Leading people in the wake of an economic collapse, COVID-19, and broken systems requires a different model of leadership. What has worked for us in the past isn't working for us today and won't work for us tomorrow. We need to see with new eyes, an open heart, and a new reality in leadership.

Let's Go for a Walk

"The greatest degree of inner tranquility comes from the development of love and compassion. The more we care for the happiness of others, the greater is our own sense of well-being."

— *Tenzin Gyatso, 14th Dalai Lama*

Isn't it odd that we say, "It's nothing personal, only business," as if that justifies how we can act in ways that are cold and aloof to others at work? How can it not be personal when we are dealing with people? People are what make or break a business. People are what leaders lead. How can we take the personal out of work?

Let's break and take this opportunity to go inward—to stop and think about how the contents in this chapter resonate with you.

- Where are you on Maslow's hierarchy? How would you respond to different people at different places on the hierarchy pyramid?

- How did it feel when you had a discussion with someone and said it wasn't personal? What felt right about that conversation? How would you change the dialogue if you could have the discussion again?

- What are behaviors that evoke trust in you? How can you demonstrate those behaviors to the people you lead?

Reflection: Where are you on Maslow's hierarchy? How would you respond to different people at different places on the hierarchy pyramid?

Reflection: How did it feel when you had a discussion with someone and said it wasn't personal? What felt right about that conversation? How would you change the dialogue if you could have the discussion again?

Reflection: What are behaviors that evoke trust in you? How can you demonstrate those behaviors to the people you lead?

chapter 3

Models of Leadership

To fully appreciate where we're going, we must stop and look back at where we've been. Leadership has been discussed and theorized for centuries from the great man theory to behavioral models. Some of the most widely known theories include situational, charismatic, transformational, and servant models of leadership. These four models have some shared characteristics with Love-Based Leadership.

Situational Leadership

This leadership model is flexible and changes to adapt to the maturity level of the followers, rendering it followership focused. The four styles of leadership within this model are telling, selling, participating, and delegating.[8] Both the situation and the followers' maturity level help the leader determine which of the four styles to use. This is a popular leadership approach with a mantra of "It depends." The leadership style one uses depends on the situation. The situation, people involved, speed, and a variety of other factors contribute to the leader's decision on which style to use.

The telling (directing) approach is typically selected when the maturity level of followers is low. The leader gives detailed descriptions on how to accomplish tasks and does not seek input from employees. The selling approach is used when employee maturity is higher and the leader spends equal amounts of time directing and supporting employees. The leader typically makes the final decision with input from the employees. Next comes the participative approach, where leaders spend a small amount of time giving directions to employees and most of their time encouraging. Encouraging and helping to build employee self-confidence reflects the participative style with both the leader and followers sharing decision making. This style requires employees to have a moderate maturity level. Finally, when followers have a high maturity level, a leader may use a delegating approach to let the employees know what needs to be done, providing little, if any, direction. Employees typically make their own decisions. This style, also known as delegating or laissez-faire, is a hands-off approach.

Many other situational leadership models have emerged; however, they do not veer too far from the basic premise of this model.

Charismatic Leadership

Charismatic leadership[9] influences attitudes and assumptions, building commitment toward organizational objectives often involving change. Characteristics of charismatic leaders include vision, excellent communication skills, self-confidence, moral conviction, ability to inspire trust, high risk orientation, high energy, action orientation, relational power base, minimum of internal conflict, empowerment of others, and a self-promoting personality. Charismatic leadership is often used interchangeably with transformational leadership, although some would argue that charisma is not a requirement for transformation.

Charisma is a double-edged sword because leaders throughout history have leveraged their charisma to influence followers in both benevolent and malevolent ways. Both John F. Kennedy and the Reverend Jim Jones were extremely charismatic leaders, influencing others toward a common vision, but with completely different personal agendas and outcomes.

Transformational Leadership

The focus with this model of leadership is on the outcome, not the leader's personal characteristics. Transformational leaders influence followers toward an outcome of change through a compelling vision. Followers are drawn to the vision and align with transformational leaders. Closely aligned with change theories, transformational leadership's primary focus is on change.

Servant Leadership

Servant leadership, introduced by Robert Greenleaf in 1970,[10] has been demonstrated throughout history by Jesus, Mother Teresa, and Gandhi. In the business world, we saw a great example of servant leadership with the late CEO and founder of Southwest Airlines, Herb Kelleher.

He was often spotted loading baggage on Thanksgiving Day, knowing his followers were working extra hard on the busiest travel day of the year. Servant leadership transcends the leader's own self-interest to serve the needs of those they lead. This service is typically displayed by helping their followers grow emotionally and professionally.

Four pillars provide the framework for servant leadership: helping others discover their inner spirit, earning and keeping others' trust, service over self-interest, and effective listening. Leaders who practice this model of leadership are typically revered more for empowering others than for their great deeds.

Hollywood

In addition to theoretical models, our society has embraced and idolized a stereotypical-type leader we see depicted in films, like the Lone Ranger. This type of leader is nearly omnipotent, strong, and able to handle nearly everything that comes his (yes, his) way almost single-handedly. He has all of the answers and endless energy. In many organizations, we have come to expect this type of leader to lead us through the hard times and reign in the good times. These leaders are expected to have strength, courage, valor, and vision. This perception and expectation of leadership is harmful to both leaders and followers because it is unrealistic. The leaders in organizations who succumb to this model pay a hefty price of isolation, stress, fear of failure, stress-related illness, or worse.

Power Models

We cannot discuss leadership without addressing power. Leaders have power, whether they realize it or not. Power can make some of us drunk and skew our judgment. For some, power is revered as a sacred gift, not to be spent lavishly. Use of leadership and power is a monumental responsibility. History has demonstrated those leaders who wielded their power and influence with a benevolent spirit, such as Martin Luther King Jr., Mahatma Gandhi, and Princess Diana. Historic leaders who used their power in malevolent ways include Adolf Hitler and David Koresh. Both of these men were by definition effective leaders, as they created a vision and influenced others to follow. The difference between the benevolent and the malevolent leaders is the way they spend their power.

Five power bases identified by Raven and French in 1959[11] ring true today. The power bases include legitimate, reward, coercive, expert, and referent. Leaders use legitimate power simply through their position or title. The president of a company has legitimate power simply because of his or her position. Reward power is the ability to influence others by offering them something of value like a bonus or incentive. Coercive power influences others based on punishment and withholding rewards. When someone has expertise in a needed area, they have expert power. The IT people in any organization with which I am affiliated always have expert power with me.

Referent power is the power of respect. This power, developed through relationships and personal appeal, is earned power. Have you ever been to a meeting where the positional leader is facilitating, perhaps discussing a new policy or change, and everyone looks at so-and-so to see his or her reaction? Well so-and-so probably has referent power. They are those leaders at all levels in an organization who get things done because of the influence and respect they have from their colleagues.

Fear-Based Leadership

Fear, the antithesis of love, has almost as much popularity in art and literature as love. Fear is an immobilizing force. Fear and love can never be experienced simultaneously. Fear seeks to separate, whereas love (truth) brings together. In times of crisis, which are typically brought about by fearful events (9/11, mass shootings, COVID-19), fear results in immediate separation. However, what brings us back from those fearful, dark days or moments is simply and powerfully love. Love *always* emerges to heal and move forward.

In the workplace, fear-based leadership is manifested in a number of ways. We see fear in leadership through not trusting employees to do the jobs for which they were hired. Micromanagement is a classic display of fear. Micromanagement results from managers fearing loss of control. I once had a student challenge me when we were discussing micromanagement in class. He thought the concept was exaggerated. I then shared with him an experience I had while working for a Fortune 500 land developer and homebuilder. We were opening up a new community in a different state than our corporate headquarters. After we selected a mailbox style and decided to paint them the same green color as our corporate-approved logo, we had to paint the mailbox and ship it to corporate headquarters so the company president could approve the mailbox and paint color! My student agreed, that yes, micromanagement can rear its ugly head when fear and lack of trust are present.

Fear is also leveraged in the workplace by choice of managers and leaders. We have seen so much fear and intimidation at work, especially with the collapse of the economy. I once posed a question to an MBA class, asking them the significance of fear-based leadership. One student responded:

> *I think it can be extremely significant. This past week something was mentioned to an employee that made them fearful of potentially losing their job. This created a real problem not only emotionally for that person, but within the entire department. The workplace has fear as a component. Some of the fear is unfounded, such as constant fear of being fired. Sometimes it is grounded because some are slacking off. That is no way to live. I am not sure how, but reducing fear is important, but maybe even more important is increasing hope.*

We must agree that fear can be a motivating factor. Fear can move people in a direction. What they forgot to tell us about leveraging fear is that using fear in this manner comes with a price—a high price. Lack of loyalty, increased stress, reduced engagement, no innovation, loss of trust, and a strong desire to leave the organization are costs of leading with fear.

> *When our fists are tightly clutching what we have,*
> *we are not open and cannot receive the gifts*
> *all around us.*

Fear and power go hand in hand. Many managers and leaders hold on tightly to the power they have. They are afraid to give the power away, fearing they will not be the heroic leader they expect they should be. When our fists are tightly clutching what we have, we are not open and cannot receive the gifts all around us. The irony of this is that sharing power makes managers and leaders more powerful, increasing respect, trust, and loyalty. More on fear-based leadership in the next chapter.

Love and fear cannot be present simultaneously. Fear, stereotypes, and false perceptions all lead to unhealthy and undesirable work cultures, robbing us of endless possibilities for innovation, trust, loyalty, productivity, and meaning.

Let's Go for a Walk

"If the doors of perception were cleansed everything would appear to man as it is, infinite."

— *William Blake*

Our perceptions create our reality. Many philosophers have espoused this concept for centuries. I always loved Plato's analogy of the cave. Plato described the fear of the people in the cave when they saw distorted images projected on the wall by light emanating from a fire. The images were frightening like monsters. Once the people left the cave, they saw reality and nondistorted images. Our willingness to view from a different lens does not imply mastery, only the readiness to change our perception. Like the darkness in the cave, when we stumble around bumping into things and hurting ourselves, we are in one reality. Only when we find the light switch in the room and turn it on can we see what we've bumped into. The new reality is that once we turn the light switch on, we can never live in darkness again.

Let's break and take this opportunity to go inward— to stop and think about how the contents in this chapter resonate with you.

- When has your reality misled you? How would you reframe your perception to a new reality?

- What impact has fear had in your life?

- What perceptions do you hold about yourself, your leadership skills, and abilities? How does this limit you or empower you?

Reflection: When has your reality misled you? How would you reframe your perception to a new reality?

Reflection: What impact has fear had in your life?

Reflection: What perceptions do you hold about yourself, your leadership skills, and abilities? How does this limit you or empower you?

Love-Based Leadership

I have never met a person whose greatest need was anything other than real, unconditional love. You can find it in a simple act of kindness toward someone who needs help. There is no mistaking love. You feel it in your heart. It is the common fiber of life, the flame that heats our soul, energizes our spirit and supplies passion to our lives. It is our connection to God and to each other.

— Elisabeth Kübler-Ross

Neither a lofty degree of intelligence nor imagination nor both together go to the making of genius. Love, love, love, that is the soul of genius.

— Wolfgang Amadeus Mozart

chapter 4

Leading with Love

Love is not new. Not a fad. Love is the core, the foundation of our very essence. If asked to point to yourself, you would probably point to your heart, your chest area. The heart represents our core. Think about what we say when we want emphasis on an important statement: "I speak from my heart" or "I put my heart into it." These statements represent authenticity, the authentic you. Leading with the Love-Based Leadership (LBL) model, we find meaning, authenticity, value, abundance, and purpose in and through our leadership. Those we lead find motivation, creativity, loyalty, commitment to the task, and value in their jobs through meaning.

Fear-Based Leadership

Before we get into the Love-Based Leadership model, we must understand the power of fear-based leadership. Fear in the workplace has been the standard operating procedure, the *modus operandi*, the way we have done business for a long time. We learn fear-based leadership and models of motivation through manipulation, scare tactics, and threats. The truth is that these strategies and techniques work . . . well, sort of.

The use of fear *is* a motivator, with the resultant instant gratification of seeing people move immediately in the direction you wish to see. However, fear comes with a price. Fear is not sustainable. When we lead with fear, we immediately lose any trust our team or employees may have for us. The lack of trust from our employees or customers leads to lack of loyalty and commitment.

Employees who experience fear in the workplace plan their escape, both literally and figuratively.

- Literally, they leave organizations for safer places to work. The cost of employee turnover is tremendous, resulting in overworked employees, lost knowledge, training costs, interviewing and recruiting costs, and loss of credibility.

- Figuratively, employees leave organizations by "checking out" or planning their escape. They become disengaged, disillusioned, and demotivated. Employees who check out are neither productive nor motivated.

Fear is tricky and sneaky. In fact, we may not even recognize the sensation of fear because we've become so used to it. We become almost anesthetized to it, all the while knowing that something is off, making us feel uneasy. We see fear in the workplace manifested through micromanagement, threats, unhealthy comparisons and competition, bullying, belittling, depression, and anxiety. So why in the world would anyone *choose* to lead with fear? Because fear is something we've all learned; we know how to leverage fear, making it a comfortable method. Fear-based tactics are the *go-to* strategies primarily because they are familiar.

The key to shifting from fear to love
is learning how to love with greater capacity
than living in fear.

The key to shifting from fear to love is learning how to love with greater capacity than living in fear. Think of a scale with fear on one side and love on the other. Only when your love for something or someone becomes greater to you than fear will the scale tip in favor of love. However, if your fear of something or someone is greater than your love for something else, then fear wins again.

- *Do I love and respect my desire to go for that position more than my fear of being rejected?*
- *Do I love and value my goals to speak up with my ideas more than my fear of stepping out and possibly failing?*
- *Do I value the call to lead with compassion more than my fear of negative response?*

Do you see how easy it is to put more value onto the side of fear? The great news is that we can learn a better way to lead by employing love-based strategies and techniques with tremendous, sustainable results that are more powerful than fear-based methods. We can learn to be irresistible leaders with the power of love.

Leading with Love

Love is our natural state of being, while fear is learned. Because love is our natural state, it is also the core, the very essence of who we are. When we fully embrace this concept and integrate it with our thoughts, attitudes, and behaviors, we come into the perfect balance of warmth and courage. Warmth and love juxtaposed with courage and strength are not opposed values; in fact, they are completely related. The root origin of the word *courage* is the Latin word *cor*, which means *heart*. We know that to be courageous requires fearlessness, and to be fear-*less* is to be love-*filled*.

LBL is comprised of three fundamental pillars: Love of Self, Love of Source, and Love of Others. These three pillars are the major building blocks for the construction of meaning, philosophy of life, and Love-Based Leadership. The love triad components are not mutually exclusive from one another. Instead they are interchangeable, woven together, with love in the center of it all.

Within each of the three pillars are seven factors, twenty-one in total that comprise each pillar. These twenty-one factors are discussed in the subsequent chapters.

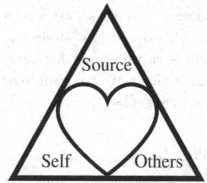

Love-Based Leadership Model—Figure 1
©2010, updated ©2020 Dr. Maria Church International LLC

Leading with love is a conduit to meaning for yourself, as well as for those whom you lead. Through the three pillars of love-based leadership, we discover our *why* and help those we lead to discover theirs. Being a leader requires us to be both teacher and student, mentor and mentee. Leading with love is leading with wisdom. Leading with love is leading with strength. Leading with love is leading with courage. Are you ready?

Let's Go for a Walk

"I believe that every single event in life happens in an opportunity to choose love over fear."

— *Oprah Winfrey*

Leading with love is a choice. And we have many opportunities to make that choice. Some of us were mentored with fear-based approaches that on the surface appeared to be effective, although they never felt good inside. Others of us may have had the experience of working for a leader who chose a love-based approach. Love expands, while fear contracts. If we start to become aware of the leadership choices we make and what is fueling them—love or ego —the awareness will be a good barometer for us.

Let's break and take this opportunity to go inward—to stop and think about you and how the contents in this chapter resonate with you.

- When was a time you chose fear as your approach with others? How did it feel? What were the results?

- What is your "why" regarding leadership?
- When did you have to get courageous when you chose love to motivate your actions? What were the results?

Reflection: When was a time you chose fear as your approach with others? How did it feel? What were the results?

Reflection: What is your "why" regarding leadership?

Reflection: When did you have to get courageous when you chose love to motivate your actions? What were the results?

chapter 5

Love of Self

In order to be effective leaders of others, we must first go inward and love, understand, and respect ourselves. Great leadership development programs always begin with self-awareness. We need to be effective leaders of ourselves, in our own lives, before we can successfully lead others. While we embark on this self-exploration, we will be making the longest, most arduous journey of our lives—connecting our head with our heart.

Intuition

We are incredible beings, complex in nature with many dimensions and layers. However, simply stated, we are mind, body, and soul. Let's first look at our mind, and how we understand and acquire knowledge. The construction of meaning, at the basic fundamental level, is a compilation of the acquisition of knowledge and experience.

Looking at two classical philosophers, Plato and Aristotle, we begin building the epistemological foundation of knowledge acquisition by blending their two philosophical approaches.[12] This compilation of both philosophies produces an outcome based on the power of intuition and choice.

Plato's nonempirical philosophical approach is rooted in a priori knowledge, an innate *soul knowledge* that humans bring into this world as pure reason. This knowledge, a priori, is independent of sensory experiences. Aristotle's approach, however, of a posteriori knowledge indicates that only through sensory experiences do we gain knowledge. A blending of both theories embraces the realization that knowledge is a holistic acquisition of both soul and sensory experiences gained through intuition (soul knowledge) and our senses.

This holistic approach of both innate and sensory experiences acknowledging intuition establishes the groundwork for the foundation of Love of Self. The knowledge that is already there (soul knowledge) and the acquired sensory knowledge together are invaluable to any leader and organization.

While we all have intuition inside of us, not all of us leverage it. Growing up, when I had a dilemma or was uncertain about a decision, my mother would ask me, "What does your intuition tell you?" I feel blessed to have been raised with that awareness. However, not everyone is comfortable with intuition, as I learned at my first corporate meeting with the president of a Fortune 500 company and several others on the executive team. As a recovering A-type personality, I prepared and prepared for the meeting. On the day of the meeting, I had my power suit on, briefcase in hand, and the confidence of one who had rehearsed for days. I remember walking into corporate headquarters with excitement and nerves. Once we settled into the boardroom, we eased into the meeting. At one point during the meeting, the president turned to me and asked, "Maria, what are your thoughts?" It was time for my moment! I sat up taller, leaned in, and said, "Well, I feel . . ." He cut me off midsentence, putting his hand in my face, and stating, "I don't care how you feel; tell me what you know." Wow, that is when I realized that not everyone speaks *intuition*. I quickly learned the language of corporate—Excel. It seemed as though anything entered into a spreadsheet would have instant credibility. I spent hundreds of hours inputting into spreadsheets what I already knew intuitively.

I am not advocating that we throw logic, research, or data out the window. Why would we not use all of the tools available to make good decisions? Let's just not throw our intuition away in the process.

When leaders and followers learn how to recognize and utilize their own innate knowledge and intuition, they can in turn elucidate those skills to others. Love of Others requires leaders, colleagues, and employees to share knowledge and skills, mentoring to and nurturing with care those in the workplace.

Truth-Telling

Being truthful to others is of course a loving action. We must also learn to honor ourselves with truth. We tell the truth to ourselves when we recognize our own imperfections. As we move through our journey, we must be mindful of our imperfections and not deny them, as to do so denies our humanity, disconnecting us from our soulful authenticity. Accepting our imperfections and taking the introspective, reflective journey, we travel to our core, our authentic leader within.

We must be truthful with others and with ourselves, with a loving spirit. Using truth as a weapon, as in, "I'm just being honest" after saying something hurtful, is defeating the entire spirit of love, truth, and honesty. That is not to say that sometimes truth-telling with others may be a difficult conversation. When a team member, colleague, or loved one has done something that needs correcting, a loving conversation may ensue with the spirit of helping (not hurting) the other person. I remember a time when I was critical of a colleague and was venting at home with my husband. I went on and on about what a horrible person this was and how she could do nothing right. "And you should have seen what she was wearing," I continued. My husband lovingly looked at me and said, "Honey, you're better than this. Why do you think you are being so critical? It is really out of character for you." His loving approach helped me take a step back and dig deeper into the real issue that I was able to address in a much healthier way.

Truth-Receiving

By being honest with ourselves and not allowing others' nontruths into our psyche, we acknowledge that we love and respect ourselves. By respecting ourselves, we don't accept others' false realities. Inspirational speaker Iyanla Vanzant[13] recognized that most of us can easily discern when someone isn't being truthful with us; the challenge is how to call them on their nontruth. I once heard her say, "While that may sound truthful to you, it doesn't feel truthful to me."

What a great line! This is so much better to communicate than saying, "That's a lie" because walls will go up and true communication will halt.

When we are truthful with ourselves, we remember our divine nature and don't let anyone treat us with a lack of respect or dignity. Practicing the skills of *truth-telling* as well as *truth-receiving* enable us to set healthy, respectful parameters in our life and teach others how to interact with us. When we become self-loving, we are living in the field of possibilities, recognizing that we always have a choice and never see ourselves as victims.

Power of Choice

Choice must be present to fully love Self, Source, and Others, making the necessary space available to nurture growth, knowledge, and love. The insightful Dr. Victor Frankl's book, *Man's Search for Meaning*, revolves around our meanings to be fulfilled and the powerful message of choice. Dr. Frankl was a brilliant Austrian neurologist and psychiatrist working on his Logotherapy theory when he was captured and imprisoned in a series of Nazi concentration camps. His notes and all of his possessions were seized. Stripped of everything, literally and figuratively, he was given a number to replace his name.

During his time in the concentration camps, he realized that while everything and everyone was taken from him, he had one thing that could *never* be taken from him. He could give it away, but he was not interested in doing so. The one thing that could never be taken from him was his unyielding power to choose his own attitude. This realization was applicable both then and today. When we place ourselves in a victim role, we are victims. We do create our own realities. As co-creators, we have a choice in how that reality looks. We can choose to create a different perception and a different reality.

Perception-Shifting

When we develop the leadership principle of Love of Self, we develop the most powerful tool in our leadership toolbox—perception-shifting. This skill will open up the world to you and those whom you lead.

For example, if someone is lashing out at you at work, really being ugly, have you ever stopped to think that hurt people hurt others? What is possible here? Attacking typically stems from fear, guilt, or shame. We don't typically come out of the gate with an attack; first we must feel threatened, and we need to exercise some sort of power to overcome the fear, guilt, or shame.

For us to experience peace instead of conflict, we need to make a choice to change our perception (reality). Instead of simply seeing the attack from someone, let's look at what else is possible? What are they fearing? Fear oftentimes can be a cry for help and a request for love and acceptance. If we want to experience peace, we need to realize that we have the power to choose a different perspective.

I am not advocating that anyone stay in a place that hurts or causes pain—just the contrary! Remembering our divine nature, we choose where we stay and with whom we interact. We choose peace, love (and okay, some rock 'n' roll). We do not need to be in a place where we are not honored.

Using perception-shifting in decision making, brain storming, and problem solving is powerful beyond measure for leaders and teams. Perception-shifting opens up possibilities. When we value the different perspectives that different team members bring to the discussion, it helps all of us see 360° of the situation, opening up so many possibilities for opportunities. Three of my favorite activities for building perception-shifting muscle may be found and downloaded in the Love-Leader Matrix™ at LoveLeader-Matrix.com.

Presence

How we show up says so much about us as leaders. Are we present in our interactions with one another, or are we only there physically, while our mind is somewhere else? I've always loved the phrase, "People do not care how much you know until they know how much you care." This is such a true statement. I cannot think of anything more loving and caring than being present with someone.

One of the skills of presence is active listening, which allows us to be present in the moment during a conversation. This is sometimes challenging to do, like the time Dave, one of my sales agents, came into my office so worked up and heated over a situation. I know good communication skills and leaned forward, eyes fixed on Dave, and nodded my head at appropriate times. When he finished speaking and looked at me, waiting for a response, I realized that I had not heard (absorbed) a single word he had said! I was not truly present, as my mind was somewhere else. In that moment, I could think of two immediate choices: (a) I could pretend I had heard and try to shine on an answer; or (b) I could fess up and apologize for not listening. I chose the latter and told Dave how sorry I was that I had not been present and asked him if he would be so kind as to repeat his story and that I would be fully present this time. He graciously agreed as I hung on to every word. When we are truthful and present, it truly does show people we care about them. As leaders, we are also setting an example for others to follow.

Here are a few tips that I share with my clients in our leadership development workshops to make sure you are present and actively listening:

- Suspend judgment; listen with your heart.
- Be aware of nonverbal actions and behaviors.
- Listen to verbal clues.
- Use intuition—listen to what's not being said.
- Become comfortable with silence, giving the other person space to think and speak.
- Practice empathy while listening.

We also want to make sure that we are showing up with our whole selves—mind, body, and soul. Don't check your mind or soul at the door; bring it all to your present state. Are you well rested and well nourished? This keeps your mind sharp so that all of your brilliance may, too, show up and be present.

Health and Wellness

Listen to your body. Love your body—it houses your soul while you are on this journey. Honor your body; take care of it. Rest your body; give it time to recharge. When your feet hurt, put them up. When you are hungry, feed your body. When you are tired, rest your body. Lay your body down for sleep the same day you woke up. Listen to that still small voice inside of you. Exercise your body the same way you exercise your mind.

We must be careful what we put into our bodies. There are so many toxins around us that we must be cognizant of what we choose to ingest. Remembering that food is fuel for our body, let's choose premium nourishment for ourselves by putting better fuel into our bodies than we put into our cars.

Like your mind and body, it is important to take care of your soul. Nurture your soul with love, kindness, and depth. When we do not care for our souls, we end up with what theologian and philosopher Dr. Albert Schweitzer referred to as a "sleeping sickness of the soul. Its symptoms are loss of seriousness, enthusiasm, and zest. When we live superficially, pursue no goals deeper than material success, and never stop to listen to our inner voices, we stunt our spiritual development."[14] We need to actively develop our mind, body, and soul.

Maintaining your health and wellness is imperative for effective leadership. Your physical body is the vehicle given to you to manifest your influence and inspiration as a leader. Take care of yourself with a power hour each day comprised of twenty minutes each of feeding your mind with inspirational or educational information, exercising your body, and nurturing your spirit with meditation, prayer, or stillness.

Listening to and honoring your heart's call honors your soul, core, and essence. When we are aligned with our soul, our spirit, we are authentic, abundant, and at peace. Meaning is not a quest but a way of life, like the air we breathe. There is no better way to achieve well-being and love for ourselves than aligning with our spirit.

Let's Go for a Walk

"Change the way you look at things and the things you look at change."

—Wayne W. Dyer

All good leadership development programs begin with self-awareness and self-reflection. I always love taking assessments like the MBTI, EQ, or Kolbe. These and others are wonderful vehicles for introspection and a deeper understanding of myself. When I do these assessments with clients, I always caution everyone that the assessments are not meant to label us, but only to give us an opportunity to walk through the doors of awareness. The beautiful thing about awareness is that we can nurture and grow behaviors, attitudes, and beliefs that support and serve us and change those that do not.

Let's break and take this opportunity to go inward—to stop and think about you and how the contents in this chapter resonate with you.

- When have you not listened to your intuition and wish you had? What kept you from acting on your intuition?

- What choice have you made that, given the opportunity to hit the "do over" button, you would? What are three other choices you could make in that situation?

- What is one action you could start today to increase your health and wellness? Will you commit to it? Why or why not?

Reflection: When have you not listened to your intuition and wish you had? What kept you from acting on your intuition?

Reflection: What choice have you made that, given the opportunity to hit the "do over" button, you would? What are three other choices you could make in that situation?

Reflection: What is one action you could start today to increase your health and wellness? Will you commit to it? Why or why not?

chapter 6

Love of Source

Source, God, Higher Self, Universe, Mother Earth, and Spirit are many ways we describe this vitality, the life force running through each of us. This is the realization that we are not alone, not separate from our Higher Power. This is our energy, our essence, and our life source. We are part of something greater, and this is our fueling station for the magnificence of life. This is where we find inspiration, creativity, perseverance, peace, and faith. This is our soul, our love, and our most authentic self. This is *the* most important relationship in our life. We must nurture and develop our spirit.

Inspiration

How do you develop your spirit? Spiritual growth and development manifest through inspiration. Do what you love, and you will love what you do. Music, art, nature, and literature are a few of the paths for inspiration. What stirs your soul? When I hear drumming—Native American drumming, Irish drumming, Kudo drumming, or nearly any type of drumming—my soul stirs. Looking at a beautiful sunset feeds my soul. Listening to music that feeds the souls of musicians nourishes my soul. Watching cloud formations or the dance of a butterfly warms my soul. Connecting with Source and our spirituality is always found in the ordinary, simple aspects of our life.

Inspiration comes during moments of silence. Inspiration also comes when we get a moment of clarity, a moment of heightened awareness, a moment of chills. Ah, the chills . . . I've always thought that is when the Holy Spirit is tickling me, telling me to pay attention. "This is a good one, Maria. Listen, learn, and know."

When you look at the word *inspiration*, it looks like *in spirit*. That is what I experience when I connect with the fueling power of Source—in spirit. This is truly when I am inspired.

Prayer and meditation are ways we connect with our Source. Stillness and silence are also paths to feeling that connection with God. French philosopher and scientist Blaise Pascal stated, "All man's miseries derive from not being able to sit quietly in a room alone." Being still with our thoughts and allowing the connection to flow is necessary to be an extraordinary leader and exceptional human being.

Through stillness we obtain clarity. When we have clarity, we have time gained. Time gained comes to us because we have a clearer picture of the problem or dilemma and see an unobstructed path to follow. As Maslow described, when we reach self-actualization, we will have clarity and sharpened judgment. I cannot think of a more cost efficient use of time. The return on investment with time spent in silence with our Source is abundance beyond our wildest dreams.

Creativity

Creativity comes in many forms. When you hear the word "creative," what comes to mind? Art, crafts, decision making, communication, decorating, cooking, puzzles, parenting? Yes! Yes, to these and so much more. Creativity may show up in nearly every aspect of our lives. Let's not limit this thought to artistic endeavors.

Love of Source or God is love-based and ever present in the Love-Based Leadership model, guiding decisions and deriving meaning in life. Love, even more powerful than fear, is imperative to good, creative decision making. Loving and leading by the Golden Rule does not leave room for fear to rear its ugly head. Decisions made out of love, made from the heart, and from the innate and sensory experiences discussed earlier, are the right decisions. I don't mean just faith in our Source, our ever-present God inside of us, but the knowing that comes from an alignment with our Source is the best possible conduit to decision making. The heart, innate, and sensory experiences are not mutually exclusive, but when acknowledged through intuition, meditation, and prayer, become interwoven like a beautiful tapestry, creating a solid foundation on which to derive meaning and creative decision making in a love-based model.

Creativity demands us to be present in the moment. My father was an artist who in his later years transferred his creativity to cooking. Watching him create art or cook was an incredible experience. His focus was uncanny, his concentration unrivaled. He could not have been any more present in the moment. He just let the creativity flow. I almost felt intrusive watching this divine magic happen. And yet, his immense joy in sharing the finished project was as warm a welcome as a sunny summer day.

Gratitude is the portal
through which abundance flows.

Happiness

Joy and happiness are gifts from God cultivated from gratitude. Gratitude is the portal through which abundance flows. I find the times when I am most happy and reflecting on that happiness, I get those goose bump chills and tickles from the Holy Spirit.

Happiness is a choice. Sometimes that statement may cause some of us to feel uncomfortable. Why is that? Because we probably get pissed off when we realize that we could have chosen happiness sooner rather than feeling miserable for so long. I think of Dr. Frankl when it comes to choosing happiness. If he could in the direst of circumstances choose his attitude, then so can I.

So how do we make that choice if we are in a place of hurt or misery? We may have to pan out and get to a 40,000-foot perspective to look at the larger picture. We know, *yes we know*, that darkness does not last forever. The sun always rises again in the morning. The storm ends. The wildfire stops, and the leaves come back onto the trees. We are never 100% at either end of the spectrum. Focusing on the bigger picture can help us begin shifting our energy toward happiness. Replace doom, gloom, and helpless thoughts with positive, joyful thoughts to further shift your energy. There is *always* more than one way to look at a situation.

I recently lost my father. I am not going to pretend that it wasn't the most painful experience of my life. My dad and I were very close and had developed a beautiful relationship. I loved spending time with him talking philosophy, art, cooking, and travel. He was an extraordinary man. As I've gone through the mourning process, I've felt extreme pain, sadness, and misery. No one has ever looked at me the way my father did when I walked into the room; he absolutely lit up! I miss him terribly. Yet, when I pan back and up to a 40,000-foot perspective, I am joy-filled and grateful that I had that experience. I feel extreme happiness that I had the privilege of calling him Dad and that I was a *Jaime Girl*.

We cannot have two emotions present at the same time, but we can move quickly from one to the other. That is what we experience when we say that something is *bittersweet*. It comes down to choosing and shifting our perspectives and attitudes. I have shared my favorite perception-shifting exercises in the Love-Leader Matrix,™ which you can download at LoveLeaderMatrix.com to help you and your team broaden the way we look at the world, to see many possibilities and opportunities around us.

Faith

Faith and perseverance are cut from the same cloth. Faith is defined as "confidence or trust in a person or thing," while the theological definition of perseverance is "continuance in a state of grace to the end." This is where our tenacity and resilience may be found. Our resilience and that of our team's is a major contributing factor to the success of our organization.

> *Stay committed to the process*
> *and unattached to the outcome.*

Finding our faith is both a dichotomous action of commitment and of letting go. Stay committed to the process and unattached to the outcome. Commitment shows up with our doing the work: staying connected to Source, doing the action required to complete the project/interview/study, whereas being unattached to the outcome is the surrender. Through surrender we are faith-filled and open to whatever outcome is possible, including outcomes far better than we anticipated.

In order to tap into our Source, we must listen and let go of control. Just breathe. I know that is difficult for some of us. We really don't control much of anything—it is an illusion. The only things we can control are our attitude, mindset, and subsequent behaviors. We often choose to stay in our comfortable safety zone, hoping to avoid uncertainty and fear. After awhile, the comfort zone becomes a prison or a tomb.

When we try to control people, events, and circumstances around us, we get frustrated because nothing is working. That is because we cannot control those things. I love the Serenity Prayer as a gentle and bold reminder:

> *God, grant us the serenity to accept the things*
> *we cannot change,*
>
> *the courage to change the things we can,*
>
> *and the wisdom to know the difference.*

Let's open our hands in surrender to touch and reach the hand of God in all of us. As ancient wisdom teaches us, if we hold on to anything too tightly, we lose everything. Our hands cannot be open to the flow of love with tightly clenched fists.

> *Our hands cannot be open to the flow of love*
> *with tightly clenched fists.*

Perseverance

Tenacity, perseverance, resilience, and agility are sought-after skills in organizations. With the rapidity of change upon us, we must be ready, willing, and able to adapt to change. An IBM executive told me that never in the history of our workplaces have we experienced such rapidity of change, and never will it be this slow again. This is a sobering thought and a call to build this skillset.

Our perseverance and resilience are so deeply ingrained in our psyches that they penetrate our soul. To build this muscle is to build our capacity of faith, tapping into Source. Additionally, our ability to perception-shift moves us along the path of perseverance.

When I made the decision to leave a lucrative corporate position with a Fortune 500 company, it required me to tap into every resource I had (literally and figuratively) to persevere the rocky road of entrepreneurship. Believe me when I say that entrepreneurship is not for the faint of heart. I stretched six-months' worth of savings into nine months and then found myself tens of thousands of dollars in debt. I'll never forget how difficult the conversation was that I had with my husband when I told him how dire the situation was and that I wasn't entirely sure how to get out of debt and make my business successful.

I am, however, a tenacious soul, and I stayed committed to the process and unattached to the outcome. And wow, I am glad I did! I've experienced great success with my business today and have had the most incredible and unimaginable experiences that I did not anticipate as an outcome. In just this last year of 2019, I had the opportunity to have a private dinner in the late Peter Drucker's home with a group of committed innovators in the local government industry. I spoke at an international conference for local government leaders on Love-Based Leadership, earned a prestigious CSP (Certified Speaking Professional) designation that only 17% of worldwide speakers have earned, and spent a week on Necker Island with Sir Richard Branson along with two dozen incredible global leaders. I can honestly say that ten years ago, I had only envisioned one of these amazing outcomes. Had I not tapped into Source to persevere, I would have missed each one of these tremendous outcomes and opportunities.

Peace

Peace is such a deeply personal state, and yet it is also collective. Have you noticed how some people can be so peaceful and calm in a storm of upheaval and uncertainty? Connection with their Source is the big reason why. Prayer, meditation, and gratitude are all conduits to obtaining a peaceful state. Perception-shifting and faith also greatly contribute to our peaceful feeling.

The prayer of St. Francis describes peace much more eloquently than I.

> Lord, make me an instrument of your peace,
> Where there is hatred, let me sow love;
> Where there is injury, pardon;
> Where there is doubt, faith;
> Where there is despair, hope;
> Where there is darkness, light;
> Where there is sadness, joy;
>
> O Divine Master,
> Grant that I may not so much seek
> To be consoled as to console;
> To be understood as to understand;
> To be loved as to love.

For it is in giving that we receive;
It is in pardoning that we are pardoned;
And it is in dying that we are born to eternal life.

Amen

Obtaining peace, love, and happiness is found in the irony of giving it away. Give it away consistently and frequently, and there you will find peace.

Love and Authenticity

When we are connected with Source, it is in our heart, our soul. This is where love resides, and it is where our authenticity is found. Our most authentic self is found in love. We find love and give love when we are authentic and true to ourselves. Our true nature is love.

In the midst of the uprising of prejudice and injustice, we are crying out as a nation and world to love one another for our authentic selves. Our love and authentic selves are found far beneath our skin color, sexual preference, or religious beliefs. Our authentic self is located in our heart center. Our hearts actually look alike. We cannot tell what color or belief system the body was that housed the heart.

Fear is what contributes to prejudice and injustice. We fear that which is different. If we want to help facilitate needed change, we must lead with L.O.V.E.

Leading

Others

Valuing

Everyone

Leaders have a hunger for authenticity. When I moved into a positional leadership role at a Fortune 500 company, I felt like I had to check my soul at the door. That never felt authentic to me, and I had a tremendous hole and desire to be whole. That experience led me to develop this leadership model based on love. If we want to be authentic leaders, our whole selves must show up. Leading with love is leading with mind, body, and spirit.

Let's Go for a Walk

"Physical strength can never permanently withstand the impact of spiritual force."

— *Franklin D. Roosevelt*

When my life does not seem to be going smoothly—overwhelmed, stressed out, not sleeping well, worried, or frustrated—I quickly realize that I've not taken the time to be silent and still. It's funny that we think that taking time to think, be silent, or be still is a luxury. Many of the executives I've coached feel that they do not have time to sit and think. They are too busy doing stuff. I get that, because I too used to have that same belief. During the height of my corporate career, when I was super stressed out and on blood pressure medicine and sleeping pills, people used to tell me all the time that I needed to meditate. I would laugh, "Do you really think that if I had an extra ten minutes that I would spend it sitting still?" Ironically, after I left my corporate career and started my own company is when I took up a meditation practice. I could hardly believe how much more productive I became in less time. Once I exercised that focus muscle, I could accomplish so much more with ease. My creative juices were overflowing, too. Why didn't they tell me that when they were encouraging me to meditate? I guess I wasn't ready . . .

Let's break and take this opportunity to go inward—to stop and think about you and how the contents in this chapter resonate with you.

- When was the last time you listened to the still small voice?

- What feeds your spirit?

- Do you feel authentic at work? If not, what is keeping you from being your authentic self?

Reflection: When was the last time you listened to the still small voice?

Reflection: What feeds your spirit?

Reflection: Do you feel authentic at work? If not, what is keeping you from being your authentic self?

chapter 7

Love of Others

People need to know they are important, significant, and have meaning. By celebrating the significance of each other, we grow and nurture one another. Through ceremony and celebrations, our own organizational stories can sustain us with a sense of acceptance. We know we authentically care about those we lead when we accept them for who they are, not for who we want them to be. Our Source creates us in perfect love, and when we are authentically loving others, we too accept and celebrate the uniqueness of one another.

Forgiveness and Trust

We must learn to not only accept each other for our own uniqueness, but to forgive each other when we are hurt. Forgiveness is the perfect form of love. Forgiveness and trust connect us. Without it, we separate ourselves from one another.

I had the great learning experience of forgiveness several years ago. My mentor, an outside consultant, and I had developed a strong, confidential working relationship. I had deep trust in him and confided about the difficult relationship I had with my boss, the division VP. My mentor then leveraged that difficult relationship I had with our division VP to prolong his lucrative consultant income. He betrayed my confidence, and I was taken out of the management role, and my mentor then led my department. I was devastated at the betrayal. I became hurt and resentful. I stopped talking to him for over a year, saying nothing to him, not a word. I pretended that he didn't exist. But he *did* exist, constantly in my mind and heart. I became exhausted carrying this load of pain when I finally realized that holding this anger was not honoring or serving anyone, least of all, me. After reconnecting with my spirit, I knew that I had to forgive him. The next time he was in town, I apologized for my behavior and told him that I forgave him for his part in reinforcing the wedge between the division VP and myself. The immediate sensation I had was lightness. I could hardly believe how physically light I felt. I was nearly giddy with delight and wondered what had taken me so long to get there. Forgiveness helps to heal our relationships with others, and it heals our heart—double win.

Nearly every organization I work with tells me that communication and trust are their two biggest challenges. We typically trust new employees enough to give them keys, logins, passwords, and confidential company information. So why do we have trouble trusting? Because at some point in time, someone behaved or acted in a way that we perceived as untrustworthy. When we feel that trust is broken, we don't go back to start, we go to ground zero. It is difficult to rebuild trust once it is broken, but not impossible.

Trust rebuilding begins with forgiveness. Ten years ago, when the first edition of *Love-Based Leadership* was released, I was speaking at an SHRM (Society for Human Resource Management) event about Love-Based Leadership. Afterward, an HR director from a nearby municipality asked me to come and speak with his executive leadership team about LBL. He said that his team met quarterly to discuss hard-to-talk-about topics. He thought LBL was a perfect fit. He also asked if I could talk about love and forgiveness with the team. I did, and what ensued were wonderful, deep, and substantive conversations. The executive team shared their perceptions, values, and beliefs in a profound and meaningful way. Team members spoke and were listened to and heard. It almost felt as though a dark cloud had lifted. We want, crave, and need authentic connections with others. Why should that differ at work?

Trust and forgiveness can sometimes feel like difficult topics to discuss, but are oh, so necessary. Organizations are filled with human beings who are perfectly imperfect. We will make mistakes and inadvertently hurt one another. We become powerful and authentically wonderful when we own up to those mistakes and ask for forgiveness. Only then can we begin rebuilding trust.

Knowledge Creation

Two Japanese researchers, Nonaka and Nishiguchi, have done extensive research on innovative organizations.[15] They wanted to understand why some organizations are more innovative than others. What they found was that organizations that were innovative had what the Japanese refer to as *Ba*. Loosely translated, Ba is an energy where creativity grows.

Great, how do we get Ba to come on over to our organizations? Nonaka and Nishiguchi continued to peel back the layers of Ba-residing organizations and found that each one of those organizational cultures lived and practiced four elements. Those four elements were love, care, trust, and commitment. In other words, love, care, trust, and commitment have to be present for innovation to occur.

The researchers also noted that in addition to love, care, trust, and commitment, compassion, forgiveness, and inclusion, too, were necessary ingredients for an organizational environment to both encourage and develop knowledge, skills, and values.

If you truly want to create an innovative organization, you've got to let your people know that you care about them and have their backs when they mess up. I don't exactly know the formula for innovation, but I do know that it takes X number of times for the innovation not to work before we find that it does. If our work culture does not allow for the X number of times for the innovation not to work, then we will stop trying. Love, care, trust, and connection must be present for innovation to occur.

Learning Culture

Knowledge, truth, and care are necessary components of the Love-Based Leadership model: Love of Self, Love of Source, and Love of Others. The applicability of any knowledge from a management perspective reinforces the concept of a learning organization. We must be learning organizations if we are going to innovate and lead or manage in the rapidly changing environment. Organizations must continue to learn, create, and exchange knowledge to survive. Organizations that don't grow in knowledge lose their competitive edge, market share, and eventually die off.

MIT Professor Dr. Peter Senge has written extensively about learning organizations, citing five disciplines necessary to have a learning culture: personal mastery, mental models, shared vision, team learning, and systems thinking.[16] Personal mastery is stretching individual knowledge and growth (like many of the concepts we discussed in Love of Self). Mental models are the ways we look at the world, which is a necessary awareness in order to perception-shift. Shared vision uses co-creation and collaboration coupled with meaning to all get on the same page. Team learning is aligned with knowledge creation, and systems thinking is how everything is connected. Dr. Senge was describing a love-based culture when he described a learning organization.

When leaders invest in the learning of their people, it speaks volumes of love, care, and trust. This is a win-win situation, as most employees want to continue to grow and learn. Our team does many training and development programs for our clients, and it is so wonderful to see the growth in both the individual participants as well as the organizations. Trust is built through this process, as well as an increase in productivity and loyalty.

Shared Ownership

How do people know when you care? How do you demonstrate caring? One way to show care is through trust, trusting others to take care of business. Giving ownership to others trusts their judgment to make good decisions.

Allowing people to do what they were hired to do is not something commonly practiced in our current organizational state. We say we empower people to make decisions and do their work, but if we are truly being honest with ourselves, employees are constantly looking over their shoulders, trying to figure out what the boss wants. Then, the boss complains that the employees are not taking responsibility for their jobs.

Ricardo Semler made radical organizational culture changes in his family's manufacturing business, SEMCO[17], now Semco Partners. He thought it odd that when fully functioning adults walked through the gates of the plant, they were transformed into children. They punched a time clock, asked permission of their floor supervisors to take a bathroom break, and did not make any decisions on their own. He decided to start treating the employees as adults (what a concept), and productivity skyrocketed. Ricardo Semler understood the concept of ownership. He demonstrated care, trust, and respect. The return on investment was abundance beyond all of their wildest dreams.

Shared Power

Power, like trust and love, multiplies when you give it away. When we find meaning in what we do, we see that our work is contributing in a significant way, making us more productive and committed to successful outcomes.

Richard Branson, founder of the Virgin Group, gives his employees limitless time off, citing that if you treat employees like adults, they give back 100%. He empowers his people to determine how much time they need and when. The increase in loyalty, productivity, and engagement far outweighs the cost of vacation time.

Reduced conflict is another benefit of shared power. We often suppress our conflict when we feel powerless. When we suppress angst, our anger can only be contained for so long, then the conflict and anger comes spewing out, oftentimes in rage. Empowered people empower others. In an LBL zone, shared power equals shared ownership. You cannot have one without the other.

Why do we hold back from sharing power? Fear again rears its ugly head. Leaders and managers are often fearful that if they empower their employees, they will lose control. Control is an illusion. I think that poor delegation skills and accountability practices keep many managers and leaders from fully empowering their employees. If we approach this solution with love to replace the fear, coupled with some training and development for delegation and accountability skills, we would see more leaders and managers successfully sharing power.

Collaboration

Shared ownership and collaboration increase engagement. When we have skin in the game, we are committed to success. When we can design or co-create how the work will be done, instantaneous commitment and engagement arise. If we are going to be part of something, we will make it work. I am always asked by clients how to increase engagement, and my answer is always the same—co-create solutions.

A major food manufacturing plant was promoting their safety culture with a contest between their American and Mexican factories. The Mexican factory won, going over one hundred days without a single cut on a finger. Wow! How did they do it? They accomplished this tremendous feat through collaboration by co-creating their solution with love.

The Mexican factory workers invited their loved ones—family and friends—to come into the factory. They had various colors of paint available and invited their loved ones to dip their hands into the paint. They then proceeded to place their handprints all over the factory walls. Each day the factory workers came into work, they were surrounded with reminders of love to be safe. They co-created this solution. They won because they chose love and not the fear of losing to win.

My team and I have been doing a lot of work with Appreciative Inquiry with our clients. I love this process, as it is positively focused on what's working well and how we want to co-create our future. Our lead trainer, Colleen, said, "When we can communicate, we can collaborate. When we can collaborate, we can innovate." I love this simple, yet profound statement. It makes me wonder why we want to complicate things so . . .

While a plethora of studies support an increase in productivity with engagement, I am sure that many of us know this to be true through our own experiences. In our current world, I do not believe there are many tasks that do not require collaboration. Coupling collaboration with the love-based elements ensures a positive, meaningful experience for the team.

Meaning

As leaders, we are bridge builders. We build bridges for ourselves and for our team from where we are today to where we want to be. We also build bridges for our team to help them connect to the meaning behind the job or task.

While executive coaching a police chief, he shared with me his frustration that his law enforcement officers were not doing neighborhood policing. When officers are regulars in the neighborhood, establishing relationships, communication, respect, and value, it is good for the residents, precinct, and community. His police officers wanted to do more active policing such as writing tickets and getting the "bad guys." We speculated on *why* the police officers may have wanted to go into that line of work in the first place. This is where the meaningfulness may be found.

I suggested that the chief have one-on-one discussions with the officers, casually asking them, "Just out of curiosity, why did you choose this line of work? Why did you choose this city to work in?" Their responses were similar in nature in that the vast majority of the officers wanted to live and work in a community where their friends and families would feel safe. The chief's questions and officers' responses brought them back to their personal "why" that they wanted to work there in the first place. The chief was a bridge builder to help his officers reconnect with meaningful work and their personal whys.

As love-based leaders, we not only find meaning in the work we do; we help others reconnect with meaning in their work as well. We are conduits to meaningful experiences.

Let's Go for a Walk

"There is more hunger for love and appreciation in this world than for bread."

— *Mother Teresa*

So many diet books talk about feeding our hungry hearts with excess food when we are not physically hungry. If this theory is correct and we look at the alarming obesity rates, we have apparently not yet discovered for what exactly our hearts are hungry. We continue to feed our hearts with food (when we are not hungry), alcohol (when we are not thirsty), drugs (when we are not in pain), work (when we are weary), and other destructive behaviors, all to avoid feeding our hearts with what we truly need. As

Mother Teresa so simply stated: we are hungry for love, care, and compassion. Why have we made this so complicated? What we have been doing is no longer working for us, no longer honoring us, and no longer feeding us. How simple is the thought that we could move from our current direction to one that does honor and serve us? Our GPS is showing love, straight ahead.

Let's break and take this opportunity to go inward—to stop and think about how the contents in this chapter resonate with you.

- For what are you hungry, truly hungry?
- What are the circumstances that keep you from forgiving others? Keep you from showing care and compassion to others? Keep you from feeling connected to others?
- How can you build trust with your team, starting today?

Reflection: For what are you hungry, truly hungry?

Reflection: What are the circumstances that keep you from forgiving others? Keep you from showing care and compassion to others? Keep you from feeling connected to others?

Reflection: How can you build trust with your team, starting today?

Today and Tomorrow

Yesterday was the birth of today. Today is the birthplace of tomorrow.

— Marvin Gaye

What we are today comes from our thoughts of yesterday,
and our present thoughts build our life of tomorrow:
Our life is the creation of our mind.

— Siddhartha Buddha

chapter 8

LBL Zone

What is an LBL Zone? Let's first start with what an LBL zone is not.

What LBL Does Not Look Like: Fear-Based Leadership

LBL doesn't look like fear, doesn't smell like fear, and doesn't walk or talk like fear. LBL doesn't simply proclaim that people are important because it says so on the mission statement posted on the wall. LBL leaders do not say one thing and do another. An organization where LBL is not practiced is secretive: a fertile ground for nontruth. An organization without LBL is steeped in office politics and scarcity thinking. Information is not shared; it is hoarded. There is no sign of spirit. The focus and vision of organizations where LBL is not practiced could read:

> We recognize there is only a limited amount of [money, people, projects, resources], and we will do anything to make sure we got most, if not all of it [money, people, etc.]. We tell our people they are important, and they believe us because they are incapable of making any decisions on their own. We are the best because we said so.

Too many times leaders and managers lose touch with their deep meaningful *why* and focus exclusively on the bottom line more than the core values of the organization. Ironically, if the focus would be on the values and the *why* of the organization, profits typically follow.

Love of Self, Love of Source, and Love of Others all require love and trust and need to be learned, developed, and present in the love-based workplace. If trust and love are not ever present, then fear-based decisions will result. Fear is powerful, so powerful that it alone creates a reality of that which is feared in the first place. Dr. Frankl famously said, "The fear is mother to the event." Once again, choice is ubiquitous, calling for a decision between choosing love to guide us or fear to guide us.

Fear holds us back from achieving so much. We are so afraid to show that we care, afraid to open our hearts, afraid that we may appear vulnerable. The irony in this is that when we care about the individuals we lead, the sentiment multiplies. When people know, see, and feel that you care—they do the same. Love really does keep on giving.

LBL Practiced Here

In an LBL zone, love of Self, Source, and Others are present. We live the words so the words may live. People want to go to work and do meaningful work in an LBL zone. A paradigm shift occurs in an LBL zone, where we discover a new way to do business based in part on ancient and traditional wisdom. In his beloved book *The Profit*, Kahlil Gibran[18] described work in what could be an LBL zone:

. . . And when you work with love you bind yourself to yourself, and to one another, and to God.

And what is it to work with love?

. . . It is to charge all things you fashion with a breath of your own spirit . . .

Work is love made visible.

When LBL is practiced in organizations, several characteristics are present. The organization is fertile ground for knowledge creation and being a learning organization. Power is shared, as is ownership of the work. Significance and celebration of others is ever present in an LBL organization, adding to meaningful work experiences. A holistic approach to life, work, and spirituality is a way of life for those leaders practicing LBL, because LBL leaders honor themselves, their Source, and those with whom they work.

Our LBL organizations trust the employees to problem solve and innovate. We do not micromanage. We support our people with increased influence and motivation. Our organizations are more productive, and our employees find meaning and satisfaction in their work, creativity, and ownership. Work becomes a loving expression of our most authentic self.

Love

In an LBL zone, love of Self is present, honoring our mind, body, and spirit.

In an LBL zone, love of Source is present, honoring the still small voice inside us.

In an LBL zone, love of Others is present, honoring the uniqueness and the spirit in each other.

Examples of LBL Zones

Southwest Airlines has demonstrated for decades that a holistic, loving focus (they *are* the LUV airline) has brought joy and meaning to their leaders and employees. They learned that when employees are trusted to make decisions, and when they have ownership of their work, they come up with better solutions than the company could have dreamed up. They responded much quicker to customers' demands, and the employees directed their energy toward innovation, seizing unique, creative market opportunities at critical times.

Semco (now Semco Partners) demonstrated great love for their employees with the change from the traditional models of doing business to an organizational culture that honored and respected their people. Former CEO Ricardo Semler believed that in order for a company to survive today, the power of an organization must stem from respect, not rules, and that the quality of life comes first. He believed that then, and only then, would profits follow. And profits did follow, making Ricardo Semler and Semco Partners one of the most successful businesses in South America.

A former colleague of mine, Michael, has told me many stories of his time with the military and how love and compassion can counterbalance fear and abuse. He described how his drill instructor had impressed upon them how they were only as strong as their weakest link. They knew this was an important lesson for their survival. Unlike some of the other units that hazed their weakest, Michael's unit under the direction of drill instructor Sgt. Johnson helped the weakest link grow in inner and outer strength.

Michael and some of his buddies were later shown great compassion from the drill instructor, Sgt. Johnson, when the privates helped themselves to some coveted ice cream when they were on kitchen duty. Once they had finished the ice cream, they found an empty rucksack to stash away the evidence of their ice cream feast. Unfortunately, Sgt. Johnson found the empty ice cream containers in the rucksack, which happed to be his! Michael told me how impressed he was with Sgt. Johnson's compassion. Instead of Sgt. Johnson disciplining the privates, he showed great compassion to Michael and the others, just like they showed to their weakest link. The sergeant knew they were soon off to Viet Nam and that some of them might never eat ice cream again. This lesson of compassion stays with Michael nearly fifty years later.

Stories abound showing love, care, and compassion in the workplace. The list of LBL-based companies is growing, including the Virgin Group, TOMS Shoes, The B Team, a vast number of small businesses, as well as many of the organizations I've worked with to shape their cultures. Now is the time to make an LBL zone the norm, not just some occasional moments of love-based leadership.

Let's Go for a Walk

*"Everybody can be great . . . because anybody can serve.
You don't have to have a college degree to serve. You don't
have to make your subject and verb agree to serve. You
only need a heart full of grace. A soul generated by love."*

— *Rev. Dr. Martin Luther King Jr.*

There are many leadership books that talk about processes and policies. Organizational leaders have been serving the processes and the policies, not the people. We got it twisted and backward, but we can certainly get it right now.

As the Rev. Dr. King Jr. said, we need a heart full of grace. Grace is found in love. Grace personifies elegance, politeness, and generosity of spirit. Our generosity of spirit is shared in an LBL organization. An organization steeped in love is an organization steeped in grace.

Let's break and take this opportunity to go inward—to stop and think about how the contents in this chapter resonate with you.

- How do you practice loving yourself? Loving others? Loving your Source?

- What are some of your stories where love is demonstrated?

- What does an LBL zone look like for you? What needs to change to get there?

Reflection: How do you practice loving yourself? Loving others? Loving your Source?

Reflection: What are some of your stories where love is demonstrated?

Reflection: What does an LBL zone look like for you? What needs to change to get there?

chapter 9

Creating a Love-Based Organizational Culture

So how does one build a love-based environment in the workplace espousing Love of Self, Source, and Others by creating, acquiring, and transferring knowledge, intuition, and choice?

In order to create an LBL organization, let's first understand the layers and depth of organizational culture. Like a tree, the culture of an organization has many interconnected components—each one linked to and vital to the growth of another. Three primary parts comprise the culture, including behavior, beliefs, and values/assumptions/ mental models which equate to the tree's leaves/branches, trunk, and roots, respectively.

When we look at the most visible feature of the tree, the leaves, we see the physical elements. These physical elements are the most superficial part of a workplace culture. In organizations, the physical elements represent the actual physical spaces within the organizations. What do we see

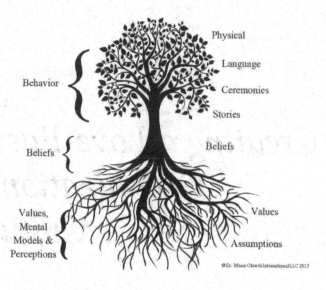

Organizational Culture Tree Model—Figure 2

©2013 Dr. Maria Church International LLC

as we approach the outward vestiges of the organization? Is signage prominently and attractively displayed? Are there windows? Do you receive a warm greeting by the receptionist when you walk in? Is the building well-kept, or is it in disrepair? Other physical elements we notice are photos and signs on the walls, mission or vision statements proudly displayed, employee-of-the-month plaques, the walls, windows, cubicles, volunteer thank-you plaques and trophies, gathering spaces, and other physical clues.

The next element we notice is the language spoken. Not whether it is English, Spanish, or some other form of speaking, but the quality of communicating that demonstrates that everyone there is comfortable with one another and feels connected. In any culture, a shared language brings people together and allows for efficient, quick communication. Often, we notice a unique slang, acronyms, and industry-specific terms in organizations. I remember when I first entered the sales field and the staff referred to the next lead (person) who came in the door as an "up," which meant to get your butt up out of the chair and go sell to them!

In our culture work with clients, we look at how employees speak to one another, how communication occurs, and how policies and procedures are written. Are they friendly, honoring and acknowledging value, or do they speak to adults like children? What does the training and development look like? Who gets leadership training, and what messages are we communicating intentionally and unintentionally? The language components are far reaching across the organization.

When employees know they are loved, cared about, and trusted, they feel better about themselves, their environment, and the work they are performing. Employees continue to grow upward on Maslow's hierarchy, without planning their escape.

Ceremonies, rituals, and routines are the next layer of culture. These elements are more substantive than the leaves, as they are thicker and closer to the trunk. Organizations sometimes strategically plan ceremonies and rituals such as annual award dinners and employee or customer-appreciation luncheons. However, routines and rituals of a less formal nature are just as solid and telling of a culture. In one organization where I worked, we always celebrated an employee birthday with a song and cake. It was our tradition (ritual) that the guest of honor cut and serve the cake to all in attendance.

Celebrating the significance of our people in an LBL zone reinforces meaning on both individual and organizational levels. When rituals and ceremonies are authentic, they thread the past, present, and future together in a culture. The significance reaches deep individually and collectively. Too many organizations forget to celebrate and honor the big and small milestones, missing wonderful opportunities to reinforce this important cultural aspect. When employees are recognized, they feel more appreciated, inspired, and bonded to the organization. Too many organizations that we work with no longer have a formal recognition program. We lose good people because they do not feel appreciated.

As the branches thicken, closer to the trunk, we think of the strength that stories carry within organizations. These stories can be stories of love, care, and pride in the organization's accomplishments or they can be stories steeped in fear and told in ways that leverage fear and manipulation. Stories told in organizations often become organizational legends.

One time, when I worked for a Fortune 500 home builder and land developer, the CEO flew in to visit us on his private jet with entourage in tow. A story circulated among the staff that he hated blue. Not a single person wore blue that day. I must admit that I found it odd that he "hated blue" since the company logo was a deep blue, appearing on all of our signage, stationery, collateral material, and business cards. The legend was so strong and fear based that not one of us tested the validity of the story.

When I started working with a client to intentionally and strategically change their culture, they told me story after story about their former county manager who was serving time in prison. I heard all about the horrible and illegal things he did. The stories were so fresh that I thought they must have recently happened, only to find out that these incidents happened over a decade before. Sometimes we need to retire stories and replace them with more positive stories. We retired the decade-old story of embezzlement and curated new stories of hope, trust, accountability, and dignity. No stories were made up; on the contrary, many great positive stories happened almost daily. What we did was become intentional about curating and sharing those stories with different departments and the public. A sense of pride in working for the organization followed, and the energy of commitment, honor, and loyalty replaced the embarrassment and shame of the past. Stories are powerful and can reinforce cultural aspects both positively and negatively.

Positive stories often depict the humble beginnings and dedicated work of early employees, shared year after year with the newer employees. To our prospective buyers, I would offer the story of how our company grew and showed them our wall of photos of communities that we had developed to "tell the story" of our company's history. This form of storytelling instilled confidence in buyers that we had experience, integrity, and credibility. In fact, we called this space our *credibility wall*.

We also shared funny stories each year at the holiday party about humorous experiences we had with customers and with each other. Stories bond people together, connecting one another through shared experiences while meeting needs for belongingness and esteem.

The trunk, bridging the branches and leaves above the ground to the roots below, are the beliefs we have individually and collectively. Beliefs are the support to the behaviors demonstrated on the surface through the physical, language, ceremony, and story elements. The organizational beliefs are sometimes spelled out through the mission and vision statements, as well as policies and procedures. Many times, the beliefs are not in our consciousness until we are faced with a situation where we must examine them.

Because beliefs are the trunk or the stabilizing factor that directly fuels behavior, it is important for us to recognize the power beliefs have over our behavior. For instance, the Pygmalion effect is a phenomenon whereby you believe your team will fail, and in the end, they subsume that negative energy and are not successful. Conversely, if you believe the person you just promoted into that position will succeed, the odds are that they will be successful. Our underlying beliefs affect our behavior. In the first example, you may not be available to the team for support, direction, and/or guidance because unconsciously or consciously you believe they will fail. In the second scenario, you may be fully present to help that person succeed, providing mentorship and encouragement. Just as Henry Ford stated, "If you believe you can or believe you cannot, you are correct."

Below the surface, beneath the leaves, branches, and trunk, we understand how the tree is nourished. The root structure is more elaborate and complex than the tree itself. This is true in our organizational cultures. The deeper we go below the surface, the deeper ingrained are the elements that feed into beliefs and behaviors. In those depths lie the values, mental models, and perceptions that are so deeply ingrained that we are not even aware of them.

Values, like beliefs, are elements extremely important to us, but we are not aware of them until we face a situation that forces them into our consciousness. Integrity, honesty, and ethical beliefs are a few values that often drive organizational and ethical behaviors.

As a coach, I usually begin a coaching relationship with a values clarification exercise. Values are foundational elements to the ways we think, act, and behave. Organizations are coming into awareness about the importance of value identification and are creating value statements to guide the organization. These value statements are as important as the mission and vision statements.

The deepest elements we find below the surface of the tree are the assumptions that feed the entire person and organization, passing through each element all the way through the roots, trunk, and branches to the tips of the leaves. Our assumptions are the most deeply ingrained of all the elements, created by our mental models. Mental models are the lenses or filters by which we view the world, and no two are alike. Comprised of our familial, educational, community, religious, personal, and professional experiences, our mental models help us make sense, assumptions, and judgments about our life experiences. For example, if I said, "pop" what would you think? Some may think of their father, a loud noise, a gun, gum, or soda. Whatever you thought of is reflective of your mental model.

We always begin our culture work with clients below the surface and work our way up. We first identify our *why, how,* and *non-negotiable values.* Then we juxtapose these with our beliefs and behaviors, working our way up to the tops of the tree model. I chuckle when I hear organizations putting a ping-pong table into the break room "like Google," thinking that will change their culture. The superficial artifacts (ping-pong tables) are only there because of what's happening below the surface. To create a Love-Based Culture, you must first address the cultural aspects below the surface. This is a similar process to developing a Love-Based Leader. It always begins with self-awareness and depth.

So how do we create a culture based on love and love-based leadership? We start with the roots and work our way up. We begin with awareness and make conscious, strategic choices to create an environment based on love and not on fear. We recognize our own mental models and broaden our beliefs. We wrap awareness around our values and deepen our understanding of how they affect our beliefs and behaviors. We strategically infuse our organizational culture with continued learning and development. We intentionally instill a sense of shared ownership and power in the work we do, providing channels for meaningful work experiences, and we wrap all of these strategies in love.

Our team has worked with many organizations to strategically and intentionally shape their workplace cultures to support their strategic objectives. Our Love-Based Culture Assessment™ juxtaposes the twenty-one factors of LBL with the seven layers of culture. We have seen powerful transformations in organizations realizing significant increases in productivity, employee retention, and reduction in turnover. When organizations intentionally shift their cultures to love-based ones, they are able to attract and retain top talent. Additionally, love-based cultures are experiencing tremendous results. One of our clients actually had a ROI over 300%.

Love really does make the world go 'round.

Let's Go for a Walk

"Customers will never love a company until the employees love it first."

— *Simon Sinek*

The feeling is palpable when you go into an organization and the people don't want to be there. Like an energy that makes you want to run, dissatisfied employees drive customers away. And you can hardly blame them. We hear time and again that "our human resources are our most important asset," yet few organizations demonstrate that sentiment with their actions. It is time to put our money where our mouth is and honor and value our most precious asset. Let's create organizational cultures where people want to be, and you will see innovation and productivity increase.

You will see turnover decrease. You will see money saved and great ROIs.

Let's break and take this opportunity to go inward—to stop and think about how the contents in this chapter resonate with you.

- What are the physical aspects of your organization that demonstrate love?

- What are the values, assumptions, and beliefs that your organization lives by? Are those values aligned with your values? Why or why not?

- What can you do today that will shift your organiza-tion/team/self from fear to love—even a little?

Reflection: What are the physical aspects of your organization that demonstrate love?

Reflection: What are the values, assumptions, and beliefs that your organization lives by? Are those values aligned with your values? Why or why not?

Reflection: What can you do today that will shift your organization/team/self from fear to love—even a little?

chapter 10

Today's Choices Are Tomorrow's Results

The forced pause that resulted from COVID-19
gives us the opportunity to fix what was already broken.

Many of our organizations are spiritually bankrupt, with zombies, the living dead, walking the halls. The grim reaper has become the HR director handing out yet another layoff notice, or the boss that is giving you yet another task because someone else has left the company. Too many organizations discourage deeper forms of communication, emotions, and intimacy, opting instead for superficiality. If we continue down this path, the same path that got us here, we are doomed for failure. The forced pause that resulted from COVID-19 gives us the opportunity to fix what was already broken.

Instead of following a path full of limitations,
let's construct a path illuminated with choice,
abundance, and opportunities.

Life gives us many opportunities to learn lessons, and if we fail to learn them the first time, we get the opportunity to experience the lessons again and again until we learn them. If we want progress and a new way of life, we must, as Gandhi famously stated, "Be the change we wish to see in the world." Instead of following a path full of limitations, let's construct a path illuminated with choice, abundance, and opportunities.

When we neglect to look at the whole person, especially the spiritual dimension, we overlook a strong and powerful resource. Our spirituality grows in wisdom, and in wisdom the world's most powerful resource is used. We can't compartmentalize our spirit; it is like compartmentalizing our breathing from our brain: impossible. And we don't *want* to fragment our lives. As many of us worked from home during the shelter-in-place orders, we got to see our colleagues in their home environments with all of the children, dogs, cats, FedEx deliveries, and phones ringing. It was glorious! We finally saw each other as human beings and felt instant connections and empathy. We laughed, told stories, and listened to each other. These were only some of the blessings that rose up from the ashes. This was love in action. As we go back into the physical space, I pray that we do not once again leave our souls at the door.

The wonderful gift of reclaiming our spirit is that no matter how dormant it may have been, you can always get it back. Spirit is always with you, and in you, and can be a force beyond your wildest imagination.

The great American professor of literature, Joseph Campbell, said, "The dark night of the soul comes just before revelation. When everything is lost, and all seems darkness, then comes the new life and all that is needed[19]." It is time for the new life.

We have to give it, share it, mentor it, and grow it. *It is love, knowledge, care, and trust.* As leaders, we have a responsibility to be students of those who went before us, stewards of our gifts and talents, and mentors to those who come after us. Our challenge is our own inward journey, the lessons we've learned, and then to return to teach those to the next leaders. Opportunities, abundance, and meaningful existence await.

Today, we need a new reality. We need to fix what was broken. We need a new leadership to shift from fear to the most powerful force on the planet, *love*. We need a new generation of leaders who have the courage and wisdom to love themselves, to love their Source, and to love others. We need you, the authentic leader within.

In the beautiful words of the thirteenth-century poet Rumi:

You were born with potential.
You were born with goodness and trust.
You were born with ideals and dreams.
You were born with greatness.
You were born with wings.
You are not meant for crawling, so don't.
You have wings.
Learn to use them and fly.

Tomorrow

Love of Self, Love of Source, and Love of Others must all be nurtured through acquisition of knowledge, taking care of all components emotionally, physically, and spiritually through learning, exercise, diet, mindfulness, meditation, and prayer. A holistic approach to life and all it encompasses (work, play, school, spirituality) can't be compartmentalized but incorporated and blended into the one being that is you. Employees acknowledged for their wholeness, uniqueness, and individuality will feel respected, valued, and loved, and in return will not only maintain and increase their productivity through motivation, but will live more balanced lives, finding meaning in their work. When love is present, abundance flows. When love is the guide, the outcomes of values, ethics, and behaviors are positive. In his book *Man's Search for Meaning*, Dr. Frankl wrote on love:

> *A thought transfixed me: for the first time in my life, I saw the truth as it is set into song by so many poets, proclaimed as the final wisdom by so many thinkers. The truth—that love is the ultimate and the highest goal to which man can aspire. Then I grasped the meaning of the greatest secret that human poetry and human thought and belief have to impart: The salvation of man is through love and in love.*

Join us, as we revolutionize organizations with the healing, energizing, and powerful grace of love.

Namaste.

In love,

Maria

Afterword

In the last ten years since **Love-Based Leadership** was published, much has happened in our world . . . and yet, nothing has changed.

When I first wrote *Love-Based Leadership* in the wake of 9/11, we were reeling from the realization of mass destruction on our United States home soil. The aftereffects were devastating on many levels—loss, safety, financial, trust, peace, faith, unemployment, downsizing, and much more as the entire globe helped us put life's pieces back into place.

Today as I put the finishing touches on this 10th Anniversary Edition of *Love-Based Leadership*, we are reeling from the effects of the COVID-19 pandemic. Across the globe, this virus has changed everything, and changed nothing.

What has changed is the global pause. Our busyness and frenetic pace at which we live came to a screeching halt as shelter-in-place orders were put into place. Businesses closed. Schools closed. Entire cities shut down.

Working from home became the norm. We learned a new language—*social distancing, flatten the curve,* and learned to use new tools, such as Zoom. Toilet paper and paper towels became more valuable than gold (OK—tongue in cheek), and dining rooms became pop-up offices.

What hasn't changed is the use of fear to move people in a direction. Yes, fear will move the masses, but it is not sustainable. Leveraging fear comes with a price. That price is lack of loyalty, lack of motivation, and lack of trust. As unemployment rises, so do tempers, fear, anxiety, and desperation.

As of this writing, what the "new normal" looks like is hard to say and will reveal itself over the next several months and years.

What hasn't changed is the understanding that we get to help shape what the new normal will look like. The opportunity to integrate the pause into our new routines brings an awareness of what we don't want to bring back to our day-to-day activities as much as what we want to keep. Practices such as cooking and sitting down as a family to eat together, daily walks, and beginning our days with mindful practices have shown us the simpler, more fulfilling way to live.

What hasn't changed is the love that we are showing to one another. Neighbors calling neighbors to see if they need anything from the store. Neighbors calling just to see how we are doing. Neighbors delivering masks to one another. Neighbors putting toilet paper, canned goods, paper towels, and cleaning products on a table in the front yard to give away to those who may need it.

What hasn't changed is love.

What has changed is love-based leadership. Many more books that advocate leading with love are now on the shelf. Dozens of articles that herald the effectiveness of leveraging love in the workplace have appeared over the last ten years in well-known publications such as *Forbes, Inc., Huffington Post,* and professional journals such as *Chief Learning Officer* and the *Journal of Business Ethics.* Organizations such as Bayer, the Virgin Group, B Team, the US Air Force, and Pepperdine University are boldly proclaiming the power of love in the workplace.

Blogs galore and consulting firms across the globe now openly talk about the power of Love-Based Leadership, leading with love, and love in the workplace as a differentiator for attracting/retaining talent, increased productivity/morale/loyalty, and increased profits. With our clients, I see the destructive nature of fear and the powerful results of love in workplaces every day.

What has changed is that using the most powerful force on the planet is more openly discussed than ever before.

Perhaps we are getting close to the time when we can say that very powerful word and it won't freak people out.

Love.

Additional Resources

For your free download, "Love-Leader Matrix™ Workbook" at LoveLeaderMatrix.com.

For more information about Love-Based Leadership, please visit:
www.LoveBasedLeadership.com
www.DrMariaChurch.com

To work with Dr. Maria Church and her extraordinary team:
www.CorporateLeadershipSolutions.com
www.GovernmentLeadershipSolutions.com
www.LeadershipDevelopmentUniversity.com

I would love to hear about your Love-Based Leadership experiences. Please contact me at Maria@DrMariaChurch.com.

Love-Based Leadership Quick Reference Guide

Love of Self	**Love of Source**	**Love of Others**
Intuition	Inspiration	Forgiveness and trust
Truth-telling	Creativity	Knowledge creation
Truth-receiving	Happiness	Learning cultures
Power of choice	Faith	Shared ownership
Perception-shifting	Perseverance	Shared power
Presence	Peace	Collaboration
Health and wellness	Love/Authenticity	Meaning

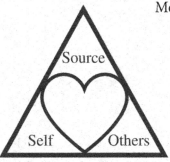

Love-Based Leadership Model™
©2010, updated ©2020
Dr. Maria Church International LLC

Acknowledgments

Thank you to the many people who have supported the message of love in the workplace—many I have met, and many more I have yet to meet. I am especially grateful to my family—my mother and father Donna and Sal Jaime, my husband Brian, and my beautiful daughter Melissa—for their support and love throughout this process. So thankful for my right hand, Marie Gacke. I am grateful for my amazing mentors—Iyanla Vanzant, Dr. Wayne Dyer, and Dr. Viktor Frankl—thank you for your inspiration. I remain in a state of awe by both the graceful dance and incredible strength of the butterfly to move me in the right direction. Above all, my Source, through which everything flows.

Endnotes

[1] James Autry and Stephen Mitchell coined the phrase "joyless striving" when describing the phenomenon of going through the motions at work without meaning. James A. Autry and Stephen Mitchell, *Real Power: Business Lessons from the Tao Te Ching* (New York: Riverhead Books, 1998).

[2] Viktor E. Frankl, *Man's Search for Meaning* (New York: Simon & Schuster, 1984).

[3] Abraham H. Maslow introduced his theory in a 1943 paper "A Theory of Human Motivation" and his subsequent book *Motivation and Personality*.

[4] Catherine D. Fyock, "Retention Tactics that Work," SHRM White Paper, 2002.

[5] The 2018 Retention Report was prepared by the Work Institute.

[6] David Sturt and Todd Nordstrom, *Forbes*, Mar 8, 2018, "10 Shocking Workplace Stats You Need To Know."

[7] Abraham H. Maslow, *The Far Reaches of Human Nature* (New York: Penguin, 1976).

[8] Situational Leadership Theory was introduced by Paul Hersey and Ken Blanchard in 1969 as "life cycle theory of leadership," which was later renamed "Situational Leadership Theory."

[9] Max Weber (1947) emphasized the importance of charisma in leadership, and later, Robert House developed the theory of charismatic leadership in 1976.

[10] Robert K. Greenleaf introduced the concept in his 1970 essay, "The Servant as a Leader."

[11] John R. P. French Jr. and Bertram Raven introduced "The Bases of Social Power" in Dorwin Cartwright and Alvin Zander, eds., *Group Dynamics* (Boston: Addison-Wesley, 1998).

[12] Both Aristotle's and Plato's theories are found in the compilation of philosophical ideologies, *Human Knowledge: Classical and Contemporary Approaches* by Paul K. Moser and Arnold vander Nat (New York: Oxford University Press, 2003).

[13] Iyanla Live! Back to Basics recorded live at Detroit Unity Temple in Detroit, MI (New York: Simon and Schuster, 2001).

[14] Albert Schweitzer quoted by Phillip L. Berman, *The Search for Meaning: Americans Talk About What They Believe and Why* (New York: Ballantine, 1990).

[15] Ikujiro Nonaka and Toshihiro Nishiguchi, *Knowledge Emergence: Social, Technical, and Evolutionary Dimensions of Knowledge Creation* (New York: Oxford Press, 2001).

[16] Peter M. Senge, *The Fifth Discipline: The Art & Practice of the Learning Organization* (New York: Currency Doubleday, 1990).

[17] Ricardo Semler, *Maverick: The Success Story Behind the World's Most Unusual Workplace* (New York: Warner Books, 1993).

[18] Kahlil Gibran, *The Prophet* (New York: Alfred A. Knopf, Inc., 1984).

[19] Joseph Campbell, *A Joseph Campbell Companion: Reflections on the Art of Living* (New York: HarperPerennial, 1995).

Bibliography

Autry, James A., and Stephen Mitchell. *Real Power: Business Lessons from the Tao Te Ching.* New York: Riverhead Books, 1998.

Bolman, Lee G., and Terrence E. Deal. *Leading with Soul: An Uncommon Journey of Spirit.* San Francisco: Jossey-Bass, 2001.

Campbell, Joseph. *A Joseph Campbell Companion: Reflections on the Art of Living.* New York: HarperPerennial, 1995.

Currier, Erin. "How Generation X Could Change the American Dream." *Trend Magazine.* January 26, 2018.

Dyer, Wayne W. *Change Your Thoughts—Change Your Life: Living the Wisdom of the Tao.* Carlsbad, CA: Hay House, Inc., 2007.

Dyer, Wayne W. *The Power of Intention: Learning to Co-create Your World Your Way.* Carlsbad, CA: Hay House, Inc., 2004.

"Ethical Dilemmas: How Scandals Damage Companies." Western Governs University, September 23, 2019.

Fox, Matthew. *Reinvention of Work: A New Vision of Livelihood for Our Time.* San Francisco: HarperSanFrancisco, 1994.

Frankl, Viktor E. *Man's Search for Meaning.* New York: Simon & Schuster, 1984.

Freiberg, Kevin, and Jackie Freiberg. *Nuts! Southwest Airlines' Crazy Recipe for Business and Personal Success.* New York: Broadway Books, 1998.

French, John R. P. Jr. and Bertram Raven. "The Bases of Social Power" in Dorwin Cartwright and Alvin Zander, eds. *Group Dynamics.* Boston: Addison-Wesley, 1998.

Fyock, Catherine D. "Retention Tactics that Work." SHRM White Paper, 2002.

Garvin, David A. *Harvard Business Review on Knowledge Management,* 6th ed. Boston: Harvard Business School Press, 1998.

Gazzaniga, Michael S. *The Mind's Past. 2nd ed.* Berkeley, CA: University of California Press, 2000.

Gibran, Kahlil. *The Prophet.* New York: Alfred A. Knopf, Inc., 1984.

Greenleaf, Robert K. *Servant Leadership: A Journey Into the Nature of Legitimate Power and Greatness, 25th Anniversary ed.* Mahaw, NJ: Paulist Press, 2002.

Greer, M. E. "Trust Seals Leadership." *Professional Safety 47*, no. 5 (2002): 8.

Hammerschlag, Carl A. *The Theft of the Spirit.* New York: Simon & Schuster, 1993.

Jampolsky, Gerald G. *Love is Letting Go of Fear.* Millbrae, CA: Celestial Arts, 1995.

Kleiner, Art, and George Roth. *Harvard Business Review on Knowledge Management, 6th ed.* Boston: Harvard Business School Press, 1998.

Kurtz, Ernest, and Katherine Ketcham. *The Spirituality of Imperfection: Modern Wisdom from Classic Stories.* New York: Bantam, 1992.

Lussier, Robert N. and Christopher F. Achua. *Leadership: Theory, Application, and Development.* Boston, MA: Cengage Learning, 2013.

Maslow, Abraham H. *Motivation and Personality 3rd ed.* New York: Harper & Row, 1974.

Maslow, Abraham H. *The Farther Reaches of Human Nature.* New York: Penguin, 1976.

Mitroff, Ian. I., and Elizabeth A. Denton. *A Spiritual Audit of Corporate America.* San Francisco: Jossey-Bass, 1999.

Moser, Paul and Arnold vander Nat. *Human Knowledge: Classical and Contemporary Approaches.* New York: Oxford University Press, 2003.

Nonaka, Ikujiro and Toshihiro Nishiguchi. *Knowledge Emergence: Social, Technical, and Evolutionary Dimensions of Knowledge Creation.* New York: Oxford Press, 2001.

Pearson, Carol S. *Awakening the Heroes Within.* San Francisco: HarperSanFrancisco, 1991.

Rosanoff, Nancy. "Intuition Comes of Age: Workplace Applications of Intuitive Skill for Occupational and Environmental Health Nurses." *AAOHN Journal 47,* no. 4 (1999): 157.

Schweitzer, Albert, quoted by Phillip L. Berman. *The Search for Meaning: Americans Talk About What They Believe and Why.* New York: Ballantine, 1990.

Semler, Ricardo. Maverick: *The Success Story Behind the World's Most Unusual Workplace.* New York: Warner Books, 1993.

Senge, Peter M. "Commentary." *Reflections 6,* no. 2 (2005): 17.

Senge, Peter M. *The Fifth Discipline: The Art & Practice of the Learning Organization.* New York: Currency Doubleday, 1990.

Starling, Grover. "Business Ethics and Nietzsche." *Business Horizons 40,* no. 3 (1997): 3.

Sturt, David and Todd Nordstrom. "10 Shocking Workplace Stats You Need to Know." *Forbes.* March 8, 2018.

Tarallo, Mark. "How to Reduce Employee Turnover Through Robust Retention Strategies." *SHRM and Security Management Magazine.* September 17, 2018.

"The 2018 Retention Report." Work Institute.

Vanzant, Iyanla. *Iyanla Live! Back to Basics.* Simon & Schuster Audio, 2001.

Dr. Maria Church

Dr. Maria Church, CEO of Dr. Maria Church International, including both government and corporate divisions, and author of *Love-Based Leadership: Transform Your Life with Meaning and Abundance*, the upcoming book *A Course in Leadership: 21 Spiritual Lessons on Power, Love, and Influence*, and co-author of the best-selling book, *Answering the Call*, has started a movement to revolutionize the workplace with a shift from fear to love.

Dr. Church specializes in organizational culture, change agility, and leadership development with over twenty-five years working with Fortune 500, local governments, nonprofits, and academia. Her organizational culture work has realized her clients over 300% ROI, intentionally shaping their cultures to support strategic objectives and be a differentiator in the marketplace. Maria holds a Doctor of Management degree in Organizational Leadership and currently teaches for several universities. She is also part of the elite 17% worldwide that has earned a CSP (Certified Speaking Professional) designation from the National Speakers Association and speaks to world-wide audiences about leading with love.

Dr. Church launched Leadership Development University in early fall 2020. This online university picks up where the traditional business degrees left off, focusing on the skill sets leaders need to be effective leaders of others. The programs for Supervisors and Emerging Leaders, Managers and Mid-level Managers, and Executives focus on bridging theory to practice with an emphasis on immediate actionability.

Maria can almost always be found with her nose in a book or ear to classic rock playing air drums (she's hoping to learn drums from Keith Moon in rock 'n' roll heaven). Splitting her time between Scottsdale and the canyons of southern Arizona, Maria continues to work with high-performing local governments, nonprofits, and private organizations. She is working on her next book about exemplary corporate and local government cultures.

Connect with Dr. Maria Church at:

DrMariaChurch.com

linkedin.com/in/drmariachurch/

facebook.com/dr.maria.church/

twitter.com/DrMariaChurch

youtube.com/c/Drmariachurchtv

instagram.com/dr.mariac/

More By Dr. Maria Church

A Course in Leadership: 21 Spiritual Lessons on Power, Love, and Influence

Discover how to integrate leadership and spirituality; live to your highest potential and lead from your highest self.

At various stages of our lives, all of us are leaders, followers, or both. A Course in Leadership bridges the leadership discussion with a spirituality discourse and prepares you to live and lead to your highest potential, your highest self. Many leadership books present concepts such as strategic planning, thought leadership, goal setting, creating vision, and motivating others. Those concepts, juxtaposed with spirituality, are covered in this course as awareness, intuition, order, intention, and relationships.

Miracles await us as we discard the models of insanity and come into our right minds through perception shifting. We transform talking to power listening, routine to openness, mindlessness to mindfulness, obsession to passion, entitlement to gratitude, obscene to grace, weightiness to laughter, habitual to creativity, disease to health, reduction to growth, knowledge to wisdom, tell to teach, manipulation to service, division to forgiveness, and fear to love.